GCSE
Success

Revision
Guide

Science
Higher

Brian Arnold • Hannah Kingston • Emma Poole

Contents

SCIENCE SUCCESS

Contents

Physics

A balanced diet and nutrition

The seven nutrition groups are *carbohydrates*, *proteins*, *fat*, *vitamins* and *minerals*, *fibre* and *water*. A *balanced diet* is made up of all of these nutrients.

Carbohydrates

Carbohydrates consist of starch and types of sugar, e.g. glucose (the sugar our bodies use for respiration) and lactose (the sugar in milk). We need carbohydrates to **give us energy**. Starch is made up of smaller glucose molecules joined together. Plants store glucose as starch. Glycogen is also a carbohydrate. Animals store glucose as glycogen.

These foods contain a lot of carbohydrate:

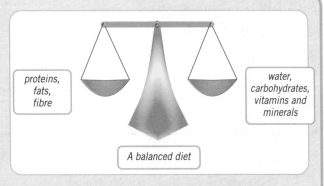

proteins, fats, fibre

water, carbohydrates, vitamins and minerals

A balanced diet

The amount of energy a person needs in their diet depends on **age, gender and their level of activity**. If a person takes in a larger amount of energy than they use up exercising, the excess is stored as fat.

If a person becomes overweight, they are more likely to suffer health problems such as arthritis, diabetes, heart disease and high blood pressure.

Protein

Your body cells are mostly made up of protein. Proteins are made up of lots of amino acids. We need protein to **repair** and **replace damaged cells** or to **make new cells during growth**.

Many diets in the world are deficient in protein, but children in particular need a lot of protein in their diets for growth.

Kwashiorkor is a protein deficiency disorder that is common in developing countries because people's diets consist of mainly starchy vegetables. In particular, they do not get enough animal protein, which contains all the essential amino acids not made within the body.

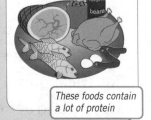

These foods contain a lot of protein

Fats

These foods contain a lot of fat

Fats are made from fatty acids and glycerol. We need fats for a **store** of **energy**, to make **cell membranes** and for **warmth** (insulation).

Fat can also be bad for us. **Cholesterol** is a fatty deposit that can narrow arteries and contribute to heart disease. Cholesterol is made in the liver and is found in the blood. The level of cholesterol in the blood is influenced by the amount and type of fat in the diet.

Saturated fats increase blood cholesterol. Monounsaturated fats have little effect and **polyunsaturated** fats may help reduce blood cholesterol.

Genetic factors, smoking and alcohol can also contribute to the effects of cholesterol and increase the risk of heart disease.

Fibre

Fibre, or roughage, comes from plants. Fibre is not actually digested, but it keeps food moving smoothly through your system. It prevents constipation.

These foods contain a lot of fibre

Water

Water makes up approximately 65% of your body weight. Water is important because:

- our blood plasma is mainly water
- water is in sweat that cools us down
- chemical reactions in our cells take place in water
- waste products are removed from our bodies in water.

The food and drink we consume contains water.

Vitamins and minerals

We only need these in small amounts, but they are essential for good health. Vitamins and minerals are found in fruit, vegetables and cereals.

Salt is needed in small amounts in our diets. An adult needs, on average, about 6 grams per day, but many are actually consuming 60% more. Salt contains sodium, which is linked to heart disease, high blood pressure and strokes. It is found in high quantities in processed food from cereals to biscuits and soups.

0.5 g of sodium in foods is considered to be a lot, whereas 0.1 g is a little, so remember to read the food nutrition labels.

> *Remember that carbohydrates provide us with energy; proteins are for growth and repair; and fats are for energy store and insulation. Don't forget the other important food groups.*

The Atkins diet

The Atkins diet is a slimming diet which suggests that eating a lot of protein suppresses the appetite. It believes that you burn more calories when your body uses fat and proteins as fuel, rather than carbohydrates, and that the body also undergoes a process called 'ketosis' where calories are removed in the urine.

The BBC 2 programme 'Horizon' used pairs of twins to study the Atkins diet. They found that the twin put on the diet lost only 22 calories more than the other twin. The programme concluded that there was little to suggest anything significant other than the fact that, without trying, the person on the diet consumed fewer calories. They also said that there was something about the diet that controls hunger.

Scientific concept

Many health scares have been associated with the Atkins diet, such as kidney problems, increased cholesterol, and an increased risk of diabetes. It was a very popular diet, but it is gradually being replaced by healthy eating plans as many people found it only to be a quick fix that did not lead to long-term weight loss.

> *Remember, each individual's diet reflects their personal choice, which may be influenced by their medical requirements or their religion.*

QUICK TEST

1. What do we use carbohydrates for?
2. Name the two main carbohydrates.
3. What do our bodies need fat for?
4. Why is protein important to our cells?
5. Why is fibre important?
6. Which type of fat increases cholesterol levels in the blood?
7. What type of fat could lower cholesterol?
8. In cold countries, what food group is particularly important?

The nervous system

The nervous system is in charge. It *controls* and *co-ordinates* the parts of your body so that they work together at the right time. The nervous system co-ordinates things you don't even think about, like breathing and blinking.

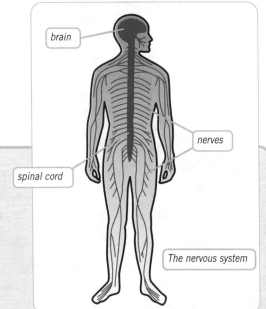

The nervous system

The central nervous system

The central nervous system (CNS) consists of the brain and spinal cord connected to different parts of the body by **nerves**. Your body's sense organs contain **receptors**. Receptors detect changes in the environment called stimuli.

Nose – sensitive to chemicals in the air.
Mouth – sensitive to chemicals in food.
Ears – sensitive to sound and balance.
Skin – sensitive to touch, pressure and temperature.
Eyes – sensitive to light.

The receptors send messages along nerves to the brain and spinal cord in response to stimuli from the environment. The messages are called **nerve impulses**. The CNS sends nerve impulses back along nerves to **effectors**, which bring about a response.

Effectors are muscles that bring about movement, or glands that secrete hormones.

Nerves

Nerves are made up of nerve cells or **neurones**. There are three types of neurone: **sensory**, **relay** and **motor neurones**.

Neurones have a nucleus, cytoplasm and cell membrane, but they have changed their shape and become specialised.

The sensory neurones receive messages from the receptors and send them to the CNS.

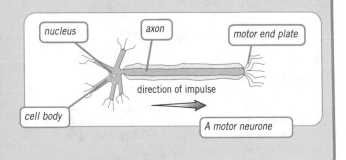

A motor neurone

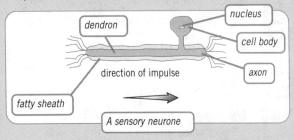

A sensory neurone

The motor neurones send messages from the CNS to the effectors telling them what to do. Nerve impulses travel in **one direction only**. The fatty sheath is for insulation and for speeding up nerve impulses.

A relay neurone connects the sensory neurone to the motor neurone in the CNS.

Synapses 1

In between the neurones there is a gap called a **synapse**. When an impulse reaches the end of an axon, a chemical is released. This chemical diffuses across the gap.

This starts an impulse in the next neurone. Drugs and alcohol can affect synapses, slowing down or even stopping them from functioning properly.

Synapses 2

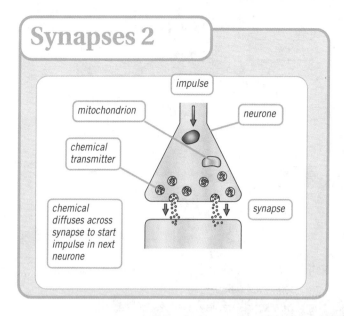

impulse

mitochondrion

neurone

chemical transmitter

chemical diffuses across synapse to start impulse in next neurone

synapse

The reflex response to your CNS and back again can be shown in a diagram called **the reflex arc**.

1 The stimulus in this example is a sharp object.
2 The receptor is the pain sensor in the skin.
3 The nerve impulse travels along the sensory neurone.

The reflex arc

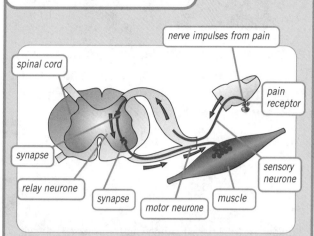

nerve impulses from pain

spinal cord

pain receptor

synapse

relay neurone

sensory neurone

synapse

muscle

motor neurone

4 The impulse is passed across a **synapse** to the relay neurone.
5 The impulse is passed across a synapse to the motor neurone.
6 The impulse is passed along a synapse to the muscle effector in the arm.
7 You move your hand away.

The reflex arc can be shown in a block diagram below:

stimulus → receptor → sensory neurone → relay neurone → motor neurone → effector → response

 Make sure you learn the diagram of the reflex arc and the block diagram. Either one may come up in the exam.

Reflex and voluntary actions

Voluntary actions are things you have to think about – they are under conscious control. They have to be learned, like talking or writing. **Reflex actions** produce rapid involuntary responses and often protect us and other animals from harm. Examples include reflex actions in a newborn baby, the pupils' response to light, the knee-jerk reflex and blinking.

Simple reflex actions help animals survive – as they respond to a stimulus, such as smelling and finding food or avoidance of predators. In certain

circumstances, the brain can override a reflex response. For example, when holding a hot plate, the brain sends a message to the motor neurone in the reflex arc to keep hold of the plate and not to drop it.

A reflex response to a new situation can be learned. This is called **conditioning** and involves a secondary stimulus. For example, the smell of food makes dogs produce saliva. A well-known scientist called Pavlov introduced the ringing of a bell at feeding times, which also triggered the production of saliva in his dogs.

QUICK TEST

1. Name the five sense organs.
2. What is CNS an abbreviation for?
3. What does the CNS consist of?
4. Name the three types of neurone.
5. What is a synapse?
6. Which neurone is connected to receptors?
7. Which neurone is connected to the effector?
8. Which neurone connects the sensory neurone and the motor neurone?
9. What is a stimulus?
10. Why are reflex actions useful?

THE NERVOUS SYSTEM

Biology

The eye

The eye is one of the human sense organs. Parts of the eye can control the amount of light entering it and other parts control focusing on near and distant objects.

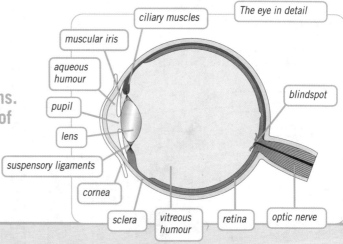

The eye in detail

ciliary muscles
muscular iris
aqueous humour
pupil
lens
suspensory ligaments
cornea
sclera
vitreous humour
retina
optic nerve
blindspot

Inside the eye

Cornea – a transparent window in the front of the eye.
Sclera – the protective, white outer layer of the eye.
Muscular iris – controls how much light enters the eye and alters the shape of the pupil.
Pupil – a hole that allows light through (in front of the lens).
Lens – helps focus a picture. It is held in place by the suspensory ligaments and ciliary muscles. It can change shape.

Retina – contains light-sensitive cells: rods for dim light, cones for colour.
The retina sends nerve impulses to the brain.

Optic nerve – receives nerve impulses from the retina and sends them to the brain.

Ciliary muscles – change the thickness of the lens when focusing.

Suspensory ligaments – hold the lens in place.

💡 *Make sure you can label the eye if given a diagram in the exam.*

Seeing things

Light from an object enters the eye through the cornea.

The curved cornea and lens produce an image on the retina that is upside down.

The receptor cells in the retina send impulses to the brain along sensory neurones in the optic nerve.

The brain interprets the image and you see the object the right way up.

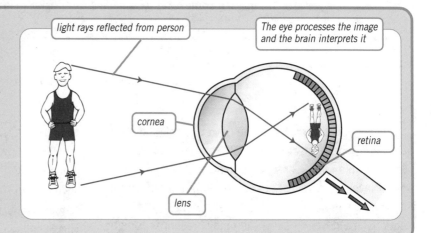

light rays reflected from person

The eye processes the image and the brain interprets it

cornea

lens

retina

Adjusting to light and dark

Bright light
- Circular muscles contract.
- Radial muscles relax.
- The iris closes and makes the **pupil smaller**.
- Less light enters the eye.

Dim light
- Radial muscles contract.
- Circular muscles relax.
- The iris opens and makes the **pupil bigger**.
- More light enters the eye.

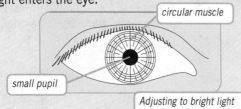

circular muscle

small pupil

Adjusting to bright light

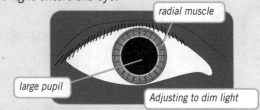

radial muscle

large pupil

Adjusting to dim light

Vision

Humans and many hunting animals have **binocular vision**. This means that our eyes are facing forward. Each eye has a slightly different perspective on a scene and enables us to judge distances and depth effectively.

Cows, horses and other prey animals have **monocular vision** – their eyes are on the side of their heads. This allows them to have a wider field of view and be aware of predators sneaking up on them.

Problems with vision

Short-sightedness results when the eyeball is too long. This means that light is focused too far in front of the retina. Sufferers can see near objects but not distant ones. **Long-sightedness** is when the eyeball is too short and distant objects can be seen but not those close up. Treatment involves contact lenses and glasses with different shaped lenses, concave for short-sightedness and convex for long-sightedness.
Cornea surgery is also an option, changing the shape of the cornea to focus light correctly.

Red-green colour blindness is an inherited condition that affects more males than females. It is caused by specialised cells in the retina, called cones, not functioning correctly. Sufferers cannot distinguish between red, green and yellow.

Focusing on near objects

- The ciliary muscles **contract**.
- This causes the suspensory ligaments to **slacken**.
- The lens gets **fatter** and **rounder**, which bends light a lot.
- The near object is focused on the retina.

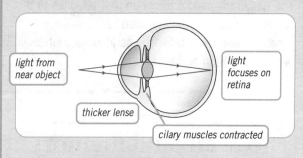

light from near object | light focuses on retina | thicker lense | cilary muscles contracted

> *Be able to describe the role of the ciliary muscles and suspensory ligaments in focusing on near and distant objects, and what happens to the shape of the lens.*

Focusing on distant objects

- The ciliary muscles **relax**.
- This causes the suspensory ligaments to pull **tight**.
- The lens gets pulled **thin** and **flat** and only bends light a little.
- The distant object is focused on the retina.

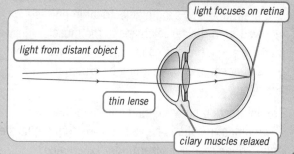

light focuses on retina | light from distant object | thin lense | cilary muscles relaxed

QUICK TEST

1. Name the part of the eye that controls the amount of light entering it.
2. What is the name of the hole in the middle of the iris?
3. Which part of the eye contains the light-sensitive cells?
4. What happens to the size of the pupil in bright light?
5. What happens to the size of the pupil in dim light?
6. Name the muscles that control the size of the lens.
7. What is the difference between binocular vision and monocular vision?
8. What shape is the lens when focusing on near objects?
9. What shape is the lens when focusing on distant objects?
10. Which part of the eye does light enter through?

The brain

The brain is situated at the top of the spinal cord and is protected by the skull. The brain, spinal cord and neurones make up the *central nervous system*. The brain co-ordinates different parts of the body to make them work together and bring about a correct response to a stimulus.

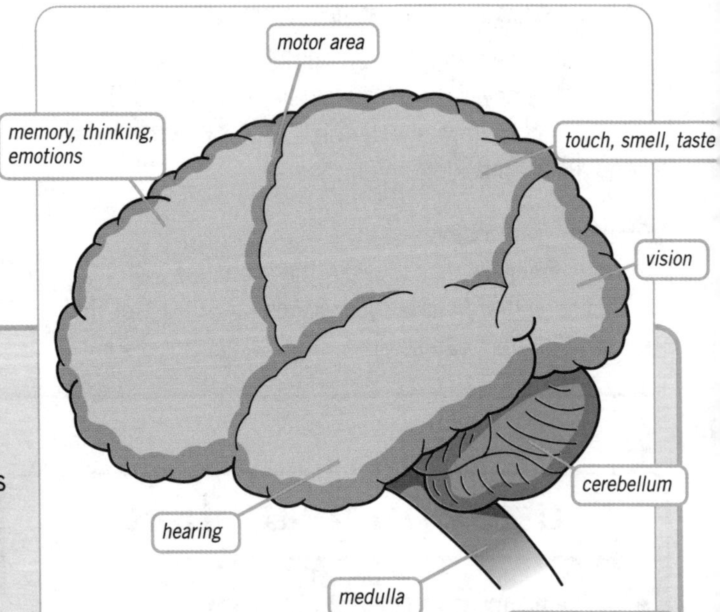

motor area

memory, thinking, emotions

touch, smell, taste

vision

cerebellum

hearing

medulla

Parts of the brain

Parts of the brain

The cerebral cortex makes up the outer layer of the brain. In mammals, as with humans, it looks like it has many bumps and grooves. The cerebral cortex can be divided down the middle into two halves called the cerebral hemispheres. These are made up of lobes.

Look at the diagram above to see which areas are responsible for each function.

The **medulla** is part of the brain that attaches to the spinal cord. It controls automatic actions such as breathing and heart rate. The **cerebellum** controls our co-ordination and balance.

The brain and learning

The brain works by sending electrical impulses received from the sense organs to the muscles. In mammals, the brain is complex and involves billions of neurones that allow learning by experience and behaviour.

The interaction between mammals and their environment results in nerve pathways forming in the brain. When mammals learn from experience, pathways in the brain become more likely to transmit impulses than others, which is why it is easier to learn through repetition.

Linguists and child psychologists are still debating the way in which we learn language. Some say that there is a crucial period of language acquisition that ends when a child is around 12 years of age.

Genie, the so-called 'wild child', was discovered in 1970. She was 13 years old and a victim of long-term child abuse. Her father believed that she was retarded and, from birth, kept her in isolation, strapped to a potty chair. Following Genie's discovery she eventually acquired a very limited vocabulary but failed to master any grammar. Some scientists, however, felt that this absence of language skills was due to her abuse and not her lack of exposure to language.

The brain and memory

Memory is the storage and retrieval of information. We can divide it into two types.

Short-term memory – the temporary storage and management of a limited amount of information. A test for short-term memory usually involves being exposed to numbers or letters for a short period of time and then being asked to recall them. The average adult memory can hold approximately seven items.

Long-term memory – the permanent storage, management and retrieval of an unlimited amount of information for later use over a lifetime.

Humans are more likely to remember information if they can see a pattern to it, if the information is repeated over an extended period of time, or if there is a strong stimulus associated with the information, such as a colour, light, smell or sound.

THE BRAIN

Biology

Drugs and the brain

Drugs, such as ecstasy, are known to affect thinking and memory in the brain. Ecstasy affects the transmission of impulses across the synapses. It blocks the removal of a substance called serotonin. As a consequence, serotonin levels build up in the brain, which enhances a person's mood.

Disorders of the brain

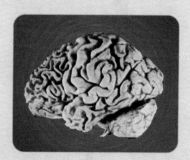

Strokes are known as brain attacks and occur when the blood supply to the brain is stopped. When neurones start to die, this can lead to paralysis and loss of speech. Strokes are caused by the blockage of blood vessels in the brain – a blockage that results in bleeding on the brain.

The symptoms of a stroke include a weakness/numbness in the face, leg, arm, one side of the body; a loss of vision; difficulty speaking; headaches and dizziness. Strokes are linked to high blood pressure, smoking, heart disease and diabetes.

Epilepsy is the disruption of electrical activity in the brain, which causes abnormal functioning. People with epilepsy have seizures that vary in severity. They prevent the brain from interpreting and processing signals such as sight, hearing and muscle control.

Grand mal seizures start in one area of the brain and spread across it. A person experiencing a grand mal seizure has convulsions, twitches and loss of consciousness.

Petit mal seizures are non-convulsive. A person experiencing a petit mal seizure becomes unaware of their surroundings and stares off into space or 'freezes' (is motionless).

Some of the causes of epilepsy include head injuries, strokes, brain tumours, or infections such as

meningitis. The attacks can be brought on by stress, lack of sleep, flashing lights or sounds, or low blood sugar levels.

There is no cure for epilepsy, only treatment with drugs or surgery to control the seizures.

Parkinson's disease is a chronic, progressive, movement disorder in which the brain degenerates. The cause is unknown. People who get Parkinson's disease are usually over the age of 60. Symptoms include tremors, rigidity, slow movement, poor balance and difficulty walking.

Brain tumours are uncontrollable growths of cells. They can be malignant and cancerous, or benign. Benign tumours can still cause problems by putting pressure on the skull.

The causes of brain tumours are unknown, but the risks are increased by exposure to radiation or chemicals, and when the immune system is weakened through illness such as AIDS. Brain tumours are more common in people over the age of 40, or children.

 Look back at 'The nervous system' on page 6 and link it with the brain structure and function.

QUICK TEST

1. What do we call the outer layer of the brain?
2. Which part of the brain controls breathing and heart rate?
3. What disorder disrupts the electrical activity of the brain?
4. What is a stroke?
5. How does ecstasy affect the brain?

Causes of disease

Microbes are bacteria, fungi and viruses. Not all microbes cause disease: some are useful. Microbes that get inside you and make you feel ill are called *pathogens or germs.* Pathogens rapidly reproduce in warm conditions when there is plenty of food.

Sources of disease

air

food

touch

drink

How are diseases spread?

Diseases are spread by:

- **contact** with infected people, animals or objects used by infected people, e.g. athlete's foot, chickenpox and measles are spread through contact in this way
- through the **air**, e.g. flu, colds and pneumonia
- through infected **food and drink**, e.g. cholera from infected drinking water and salmonella poisoning from infected food.

Disease can be non-infectious and caused by vitamin deficiencies such as scurvy (lack of vitamin C), mineral deficiencies such as anaemia (lack of iron), or body disorders like cancer or diabetes. Other disorders can be inherited, like red-green colour blindness or diabetes.

 Remember that not all microbes are harmful and cause disease.

Cancer

Cancer occurs when body cells that are normally under control, grow out of control and become a mass of cells known as a tumour. If the tumour stops growing it is known as 'benign', and is not usually dangerous. However, some tumours continue to grow and invade the surrounding tissues and organs. This is called a malignant tumour and is dangerous.

The most common cancer in men is prostate cancer. In most cases, if it is caught early enough it can be cured.

There is some evidence that eating a low fat diet and taking the supplement selenium reduces the risk.

Breast cancer may affect up to one in nine women in their life and 1% of males. It often runs in families. Taking the contraceptive pill, obesity and heavy drinking increase the risk.

Skin cancer is caused by the overexposure to ultraviolet light from sunlight or sun beds. The risk is increased for people with fair skin and a lot of moles.

Tuberculosis

Tuberculosis, or TB, is an infectious disease affecting the lungs, which results in bacteria destroying the lung tissue. It is spread when sufferers of the disease cough and sneeze, causing other people to breathe in the bacterial TB.

TB was a major problem in the early 19th and 20th centuries. In the 1940s, improvements to public health and the discovery of an antibiotic to treat it, led to a decline of the infection. For a while, however, the guard was let down and incidences of the disease increased again in the 1980s, particularly as drug-resistant strains began to emerge. There are about 7000 cases reported in the UK at present.

Treatment involves a course of antibiotics. Various antibiotics are used to prevent the bacteria from becoming resistant to one type. Schools have a vaccine called the BCG to prevent TB.

Fungi

Fungi cause diseases such as athlete's foot and ringworm. Fungi reproduce by **making spores** that can be carried from person to person. Most fungi are useful as decomposers. Yeast is a fungus that is used when making bread, beer and wine.

Bacteria

Bacteria are living organisms that feed, move and carry out respiration.

How bacteria cause disease
Bacteria **destroy living tissue**. For example, tuberculosis **destroys lung tissue**.

Bacteria can produce poisons, called toxins. For example, food poisoning is caused by bacteria releasing **toxins**.

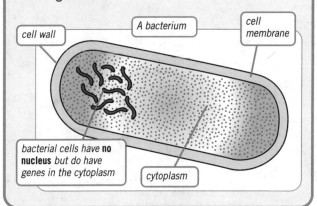

cell wall

A bacterium

cell membrane

bacterial cells have **no nucleus** but do have genes in the cytoplasm

cytoplasm

Viruses

Viruses consist of a **protein coat** surrounding a few **genes**.

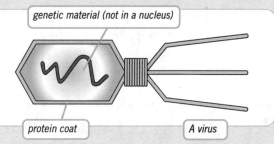

genetic material (not in a nucleus)

protein coat

A virus

Viruses are much smaller than bacteria. They don't feed, move, respire or grow: they just reproduce. Viruses can only survive inside the cells of a living organism. They **reproduce inside the cells** and release thousands of new viruses to infect new cells. They **kill the cell** in the process. Examples of diseases caused by viruses are HIV, flu, chickenpox and measles.

> *Learn the structure of a bacterium and a virus: notice the similarities and differences between these and general animal and plant cells.*

How do pathogens get in?

Pathogens have to enter our body before they can do any harm.

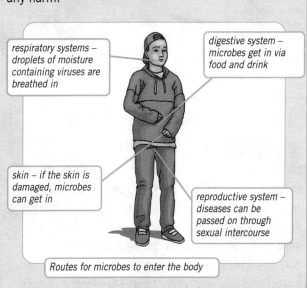

respiratory systems – droplets of moisture containing viruses are breathed in

digestive system – microbes get in via food and drink

skin – if the skin is damaged, microbes can get in

reproductive system – diseases can be passed on through sexual intercourse

Routes for microbes to enter the body

Symptoms of infection

Symptoms are the effects diseases have on the body: they are usually caused by the toxins released by the pathogens. Symptoms include a high temperature, headache, loss of appetite and sickness.

Vectors

Some pathogens rely on **vectors** to transfer them from one organism to another. A vector is an organism that transports a pathogen. An example would be a **mosquito**.

A mosquito carrying the parasite that causes malaria may infect another person by injecting the parasite into the person's bloodstream when it bites them.

A parasite is an organism that lives off another without any benefit to the host.

QUICK TEST

 1   Name the three types of microbe.

 2   What do we call microbes that cause disease?

 3   How do bacteria cause disease?

 4   How do viruses cause disease?

5   Give two examples of diseases caused by fungi.

 6   How are infections spread?

 7   What is a vector? Give an example.

8   Name three ways in which pathogens can enter the body.

Defence against disease

The human body has many methods of *preventing pathogens* from entering the body. If pathogens do get into the body, however, your *immune system* goes into action.

Prevention is better than cure

The human body has several ways of preventing disease-causing microbes from entering: these are called natural defences.

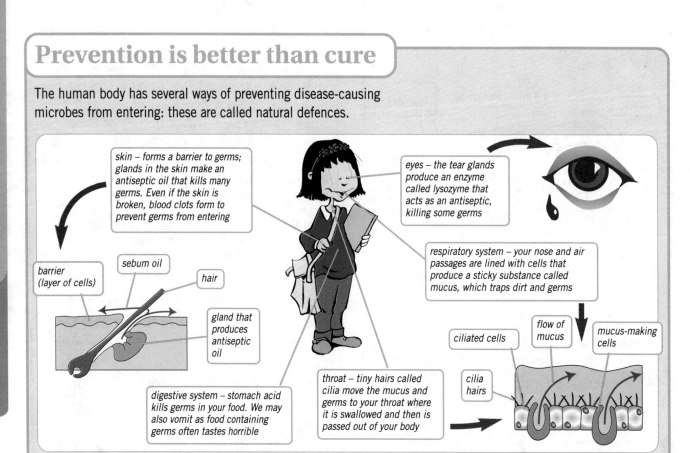

skin – forms a barrier to germs; glands in the skin make an antiseptic oil that kills many germs. Even if the skin is broken, blood clots form to prevent germs from entering

eyes – the tear glands produce an enzyme called lysozyme that acts as an antiseptic, killing some germs

respiratory system – your nose and air passages are lined with cells that produce a sticky substance called mucus, which traps dirt and germs

barrier (layer of cells)

sebum oil

hair

gland that produces antiseptic oil

flow of mucus

ciliated cells

mucus-making cells

digestive system – stomach acid kills germs in your food. We may also vomit as food containing germs often tastes horrible

throat – tiny hairs called cilia move the mucus and germs to your throat where it is swallowed and then is passed out of your body

cilia hairs

Antibiotics

Sometimes bacteria get through the body's defences and reproduce successfully. In this case, outside help in the form of **antibiotics** is needed to kill the germs. Antibiotics kill the germs without harming the body cells.

Penicillin was the first form of antibiotic. It is made from a mould called *Penicillium notatum*. **Antibiotics cannot treat infections caused by viruses**. The body has to fight them on its own. Antibiotics can kill most bacteria, but as we continue to use them, bacteria are becoming **resistant** to them. New antibiotics are constantly needed to fight the battle against bacteria.

There are no drugs to kill viruses. You just have to wait for your body to deal with them. There is a need for careful use of antibiotics as overuse has led to the highly resistant MRSA developing.

The immune system response

If pathogens get into your body, **white blood cells** travelling around in your blood spring into action. White blood cells can make chemicals called **antitoxins** that destroy the toxins produced by bacteria. White blood cells called **phagocytes** try to engulf bacteria or viruses before they have a chance to do any harm. If the pathogens occur in large numbers, the other type of white blood cell, called **lymphocytes**, are involved.

All germs have chemicals on their surface called antigens. Lymphocytes recognise these antigens as foreign. **Lymphocytes produce chemicals called antibodies** that attach to these antigens and clump them together. **Phagocytes** can then engulf and destroy the bacteria and viruses.

Artificial immunity

Artificial immunity involves the use of vaccines. **A vaccine contains dead or harmless germs**. These germs still have antigens in them and your white blood cells respond to them as if they were alive, by multiplying and producing antibodies. A vaccine is an advanced warning so that, if the person is infected by the germ, the white blood cells can **respond immediately** and kill them.

Vaccinations are an example of **passive immunity** as you produce your own antibodies and are fighting the disease yourself. An injection of ready-made antibodies is called **active immunity**.

Vaccines help prevent the spread of disease and epidemics, but it is each person's choice to decide whether to have vaccinations for themselves or their children.

The vaccine to treat MMR (measles, mumps and rubella) is a viral vaccine. It has recently caused

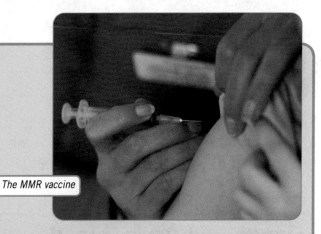
The MMR vaccine

controversy because of the possible side effects of using a triple vaccine instead of three separate ones. All vaccines, in fact, carry the possibility of side effects.

New vaccines against flu are needed regularly as the virus changes so often. HIV vaccines are also a problem as the virus has a high mutation rate and damages the immune system.

 Make sure you know the difference between natural immunity and artificial immunity.

Drug testing

New drugs and medical treatments have to be extensively tested and trialled before being used. They are tested in the laboratory before being tested on human volunteers. They are first tested on healthy volunteers to test for safety and then people with the illness to test for effectiveness. The tests are normally conducted 'blind' or 'double blind', where neither the patients nor the doctors know who is being treated with the new drug. The patients will still receive the normal treatment for their disease. Placebos (a dummy drug, which is given to a control group) are not often used, as patients must still receive treatment. Sometimes the tests fail, as in the case of **thalidomide**, a drug originally developed as a sleeping pill. It was found to be effective at treating morning sickness: it

had not, however, been tested for this use. The drug caused abnormalities in babies born to mothers taking the drug and was then banned. More recently, it has been used to treat leprosy.

Natural immunity

Making antibodies takes time, which is why you feel ill at first and then get better as the disease is destroyed by the white blood cells and antibodies.

Once a particular antibody is made, it stays in your body. If the same disease enters your body again, the antibodies are much quicker at destroying it and you feel no symptoms.

You are now immune to that disease.

QUICK TEST

1. How does the skin protect against disease?
2. What is the job of mucus?
3. Name the two types of white blood cell that are involved in the immune response.
4. What chemicals do white blood cells produce?
5. What do antitoxins do?
6. What is the role of antibodies?
7. What are vaccines?
8. What are antibiotics and why are we always looking for new types?

Drugs

Smoking and solvents damage health, without a doubt. Alcohol and drugs are also dangerous if misused, for either recreational or pharmaceutical purposes.

Drugs – why are they dangerous?

Drugs are powerful chemicals: they alter the way the body works, often without you realising it. There are useful drugs such as penicillin and antibiotics, but these can be dangerous if misused.

Some drugs affect the brain and nervous system, which in turn affect activities such as driving and behaviour. They also affect different people in many different ways: you can never be sure what will happen. It is often difficult to tell how strong a drug is or how much to take and so accidental overdoses can easily occur.

Drugs fall into four main groups: sedatives, painkillers, hallucinogens, and stimulants.

Sedatives

These drugs **slow down the brain** and make you feel sleepy. Barbiturates, which are powerful sedatives, are used as anaesthetics in hospitals.

These drugs seriously alter reaction times and give you poor judgement of speed and distances.

Painkillers

These drugs **suppress the pain sensors in the brain**. Aspirin, heroin and morphine are examples.

Hallucinogens

These drugs make you see or hear things that don't exist. These imaginings are called hallucinations. Examples of hallucinogens are ecstasy, LSD and cannabis.

Stimulants

These drugs **speed up the brain and nervous system** and make you more alert and awake. Examples include amphetamines, cocaine, and the less harmful caffeine in tea and coffee.

Concentrate on the health problems for the exam, but the social aspects are still important.

Alcohol

Alcohol is a legal and socially acceptable drug, but it can still cause a lot of harm. It is a **depressant** and reduces the activity of the brain and nervous system. Absorbed through the gut and taken to the brain in the blood, alcohol damages neurones in the brain and can cause irreversible brain damage. The liver breaks down alcohol at the rate of one unit an hour, but an excess of alcohol has a very **damaging effect on the liver, called cirrhosis**. Increasing amounts of alcohol cause people to lose control and slur their words. In this state, accidents are more likely to happen. Alcohol can become very addictive without the person thinking they have a problem.

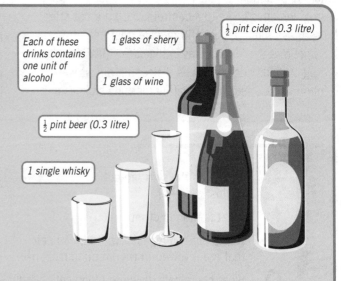

Each of these drinks contains one unit of alcohol

1 glass of sherry

½ pint cider (0.3 litre)

1 glass of wine

½ pint beer (0.3 litre)

1 single whisky

Solvents

Solvents include everyday products like glue and aerosols. The fumes are inhaled and are absorbed by the lungs. They soon reach the brain and **slow down breathing and heart rates**. Solvents also damage the **kidneys and liver**. Repeated inhalation can cause loss of control and unconsciousness.

First-time inhalers often die from heart failure or suffocation if using aerosols. Many of the symptoms are similar to being drunk: vomiting may occur and the person may not be in control.

Solvents, like glue and aerosols, reach the brain

Smoking

Without a doubt, tobacco causes health problems. It contains many harmful chemicals: **nicotine** is an addictive substance and a mild stimulant; **tar** is known to contain carcinogens that contribute to cancer; and carbon monoxide prevents the red blood cells from carrying oxygen. If pregnant women smoke, **carbon monoxide** deprives the foetus of oxygen and can lead to a low birth mass. Some of the diseases aggravated by smoking include **emphysema**, **bronchitis**, **heart and blood vessel problems** and **lung cancer**.

As well as health problems, there is also the high cost of smoking and the negative social aspects. The link between smoking and lung cancer is now widely accepted. According to Cancer Research UK it causes 9 out of 10 lung cancers.

Smoking: a proven cause of health problems

Drugs and the Law

Drugs are classified in law as Class A, Class B and Class C. Class A drugs, such as heroin, carry the most severe penalties if you are caught with it in your possession. Supply of the drug can lead to life imprisonment. Class B drugs, such as amphetamines, still carry severe penalties of up to 14 years imprisonment. Recently, cannabis has become a Class C drug carrying less harsh penalties if you are caught with it in your possession. If, however, it is considered to be 'possession with intent to supply', the penalty is up to 14 years imprisonment.

The debate still continues about whether cannabis is harmful and addictive or whether it leads on to harder drugs such as heroin. At present, health professionals cannot agree. It is said to be psychologically addictive, however, and if taken with nicotine, the nicotine makes it physically addictive. Some people argue that it is a useful pain-relief drug for the terminally ill, but medical opinion on this fluctuates.

QUICK TEST

1. Which parts of the body are affected by alcohol?
2. What are stimulants?
3. Name three chemicals contained in tobacco.
4. What diseases does smoking aggravate?
5. What is the name of the disease of the liver?
6. What do painkillers do?
7. Which drugs slow down the brain?

Hormones and diabetes

Hormones are *chemical messengers* produced by glands known as endocrine glands. Hormones *travel in the blood* to target organs. *Diabetes* is a disease caused by too little of the hormone insulin.

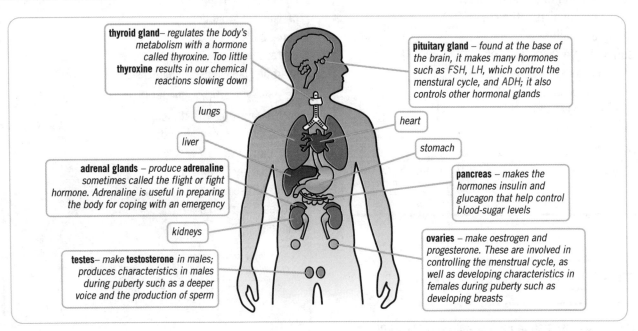

thyroid gland– *regulates the body's metabolism with a hormone called thyroxine. Too little* **thyroxine** *results in our chemical reactions slowing down*

lungs

liver

adrenal glands – *produce* **adrenaline** *sometimes called the flight or fight hormone. Adrenaline is useful in preparing the body for coping with an emergency*

kidneys

testes– *make* **testosterone** *in males; produces characteristics in males during puberty such as a deeper voice and the production of sperm*

pituitary gland – *found at the base of the brain, it makes many hormones such as FSH, LH, which control the menstural cycle, and ADH; it also controls other hormonal glands*

heart

stomach

pancreas – *makes the hormones insulin and glucagon that help control blood-sugar levels*

ovaries – *make oestrogen and progesterone. These are involved in controlling the menstrual cycle, as well as developing characteristics in females during puberty such as developing breasts*

Diabetes

Diabetes results when the **pancreas does not make enough of the hormone insulin**. As a consequence, blood sugar levels rise and very little glucose is absorbed by the cells for respiration. This can make the sufferer tired and thirsty. If untreated, it leads to weight loss and even death.

Diabetes can be controlled in two ways:

1 **Attention to diet**: a special low-glucose diet is needed and can be all that is needed to control some diabetes.

2 In more severe cases, diabetics have to **inject themselves with insulin** before meals. This causes the liver to convert the glucose into glycogen straight away, thus removing glucose from the blood.

Scientific concept

In 1920, Fred Banting and Charles Best discovered insulin as a treatment for diabetes. They extracted it from the pancreas and successfully treated diabetic dogs. We used to use pig's insulin to treat diabetes in humans.

Hormone action

■ Hormones are just one way of transmitting information from place to place within the body.

■ Hormonal effects tend to be **slower, long lasting** and **can affect a number of organs**, as is the case for adrenaline.

■ Nervous control is **much quicker**, as in the reflex response, but its effects **don't last very long**. Nervous control is also **confined to a particular area** of the body.

Pancreas and homeostasis

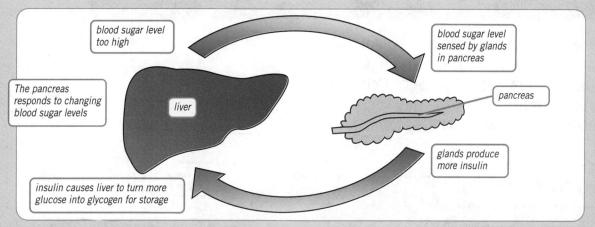

blood sugar level too high

The pancreas responds to changing blood sugar levels

liver

insulin causes liver to turn more glucose into glycogen for storage

blood sugar level sensed by glands in pancreas

pancreas

glands produce more insulin

Homeostasis is the mechanism by which the body **maintains normal levels**, such as temperature and control of body water, by making constant adjustments. The pancreas is an organ involved in homeostasis: it **maintains the level of glucose (sugar) in the blood** so that there is enough for respiration. The pancreas secretes two hormones into the blood, **insulin and glucagon**. If blood sugar levels are **too high**, which could be the case after a high carbohydrate meal, special cells in the pancreas detect these changes and release insulin. The **liver** responds to the amount of insulin in the blood and takes up glucose and **stores it as glycogen. Blood sugar levels return to normal**.

If blood sugar levels are **too low**, which could be the case during exercise, the pancreas secretes **glucagon**. **Glucagon** stimulates the **conversion of stored glycogen in the liver back into glucose** which is released into the blood. **Blood sugar levels return to normal**. Homeostasis involves many other organs of the body, such as the skin and kidneys, in working together to maintain internal conditions, such as balancing water loss with water gain, the ion content, and temperature.

Remember, insulin lowers blood sugar levels and glucagon raises blood sugar levels.

Negative feedback

Negative feedback is involved in all homeostatic mechanisms. The pancreas controls blood sugar levels using this mechanism.

Look at the diagram on the right to see how it works.

It is common for people to confuse glycogen (storage glucose) with glucagon (the hormone). Make sure you know the difference.

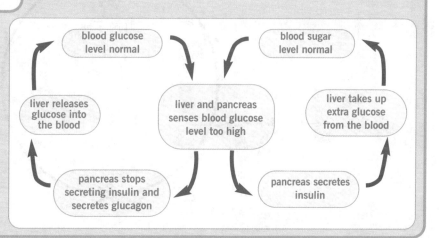

blood glucose level normal

blood sugar level normal

liver releases glucose into the blood

liver and pancreas senses blood glucose level too high

liver takes up extra glucose from the blood

pancreas stops secreting insulin and secretes glucagon

pancreas secretes insulin

QUICK TEST

1. Which glands secrete adrenaline?
2. Which gland is involved in control of the menstrual cycle?
3. What is homeostasis?
4. What two hormones does the pancreas produce?
5. What does the liver do with excess glucose?
6. Which hormone raises blood sugar levels?
7. Which hormone lowers blood sugar levels?
8. What causes diabetes?
9. How can diabetes be treated?

The menstrual cycle

The menstrual cycle lasts approximately *28 days*. It consists of a *menstrual bleed and ovulation*, the release of an egg. *Hormones* control the whole cycle. Ovaries secrete the hormones *progesterone* and *oestrogen*.

fallopian tube

ovary

uterus

ovary

uterus lining

cervix

vagina

Hormones

Hormones are chemicals released from glands in the body straight into the bloodstream. The effects of hormones are slower than the nervous messages but longer lasting. They control things that need constant adjustment.

The male and female sex hormones control characteristics during puberty. In males, the voice breaks, they develop hair on their face and body, the genitals develop and sperm production begins. In females, the breasts develop, they grow hair under the arms and pubic hair, and menstruation starts.

The stages of the menstrual cycle

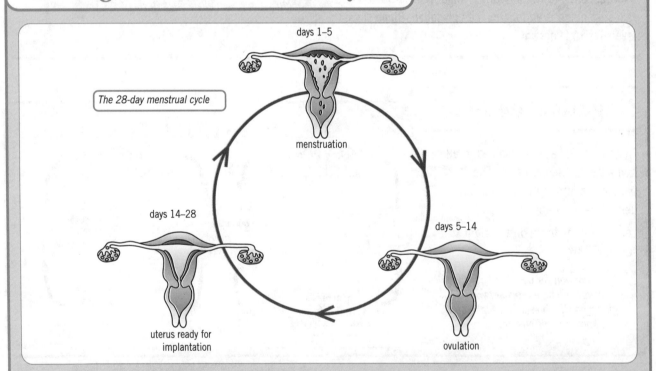

days 1–5

The 28-day menstrual cycle

menstruation

days 14–28

days 5–14

uterus ready for implantation

ovulation

Days 1–5 – a menstrual bleed (a period) occurs: the lining of the uterus breaks down. This is **caused by lack of progesterone**.

Days 5–14 – oestrogen is released from the ovaries and the uterus lining builds up again. Oestrogen also stimulates egg development and release of the egg from the ovaries, which is called **ovulation**.

Days 14–28 – **progesterone** is released, which maintains the uterus lining. If no fertilisation occurs then **progesterone production stops**.

Days 28–5 – the cycle begins again.

The pituitary gland

The two hormones released from the ovaries are controlled by the **pituitary gland** situated at the base of the brain. The pituitary gland secretes two more hormones, the follicle stimulating hormone and luteinising hormone. There is no need to learn how to spell them as they can be written as **FSH** and **LH**.

Follow the diagram below to see how the hormones interact to control the menstrual cycle.

Progesterone is released, which maintains the uterus lining.

Oestrogen also keeps the uterus lining thick and ready for pregnancy.

If no pregnancy occurs, progesterone production stops and the cycle begins again.

> *The role of the hormones in controlling the menstrual cycle is a favourite for the exam.*

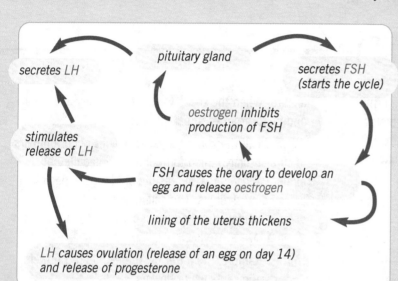

pituitary gland

secretes LH

secretes FSH (starts the cycle)

oestrogen inhibits production of FSH

stimulates release of LH

FSH causes the ovary to develop an egg and release oestrogen

lining of the uterus thickens

LH causes ovulation (release of an egg on day 14) and release of progesterone

Controlling fertility

Fertility in women can be controlled in two ways:

1 FSH can be administered as a **'fertility drug'** to women whose own production is too low to stimulate eggs to mature. This can result in multiple births.

2 Oestrogen can be used as an **oral contraceptive** to inhibit FSH so that no eggs mature.

IVF is a treatment for infertile couples. It involves extracting the eggs and sperm and fertilising them outside the body. The cells that develop are then implanted in the womb for growth and development into an embryo.

> *Be prepared to evaluate the benefits and problems associated with the use of hormones to control fertility. For example, do they interfere with nature? Or are the possible side effects they may cause a risk worth taking?*

QUICK TEST

1. On what days does the menstrual bleed usually take place?

2. What causes the uterus lining to break down?

3. Where are the hormones oestrogen and progesterone made?

4. From where are the eggs released?

5. Although oestrogen is stated as stimulating egg release, this is actually caused by another hormone. Which one?

6. Which two hormones are produced by the pituitary gland?

7. What two things does the follicle stimulating hormone do?

8. Which two hormones maintain the uterus lining?

9. What is ovulation?

10. How long is the average menstrual cycle?

Genetics and variation

Genetics is the study of how information is passed on from generation to generation. Genetic diagrams are used to show how certain characteristics are passed on. All living things vary in the way they look and behave. Genetics, the environment, or a combination of both, may cause variation.

Mendel's experiments

Gregor Mendel, an Austrian monk, discovered the principle behind genetics by studying the inheritance of a single factor in pea plants. The inheritance of single characteristics is called **monohybrid inheritance**.

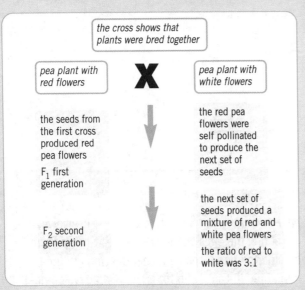

the cross shows that plants were bred together

pea plant with red flowers **X** pea plant with white flowers

the seeds from the first cross produced red pea flowers

F_1 first generation

the red pea flowers were self pollinated to produce the next set of seeds

F_2 second generation

the next set of seeds produced a mixture of red and white pea flowers

the ratio of red to white was 3:1

He bred a **pure breeding, red pea plant with a pure breeding, white pea plant** and found that they always produced red flowers (the **F_1 generation**). He named the red feature the **dominant** characteristic. When he bred two of the red pea plants together, he discovered that the next set of flowers were a mixture of red and white pea flowers (the **F_2 generation**). The **ratio** of red to white was **3 : 1**. Mendel called the white characteristic **recessive**. From his experiments, Mendel concluded that the peas must carry **a pair of factors for each**

feature. When the seeds were formed, they inherited one factor from each parent at random.

We now call these factors **genes**. Genes occur on **pairs of chromosomes**. Each form of a gene is called an **allele**. We can show the results of Mendel's pea plant cross using symbols. The **dominant** characteristic is given a **capital letter** and the **recessive** characteristic is given a **lower-case letter**.

In this example, the letter 'R' represents red flowers and 'r' represents white flowers.

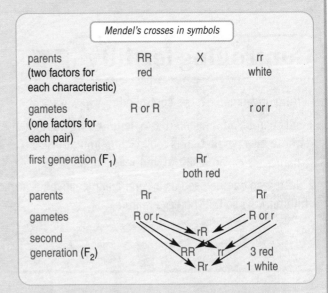

Mendel's crosses in symbols

parents (two factors for each characteristic)	RR red	X	rr white
gametes (one factors for each pair)	R or R		r or r
first generation (F_1)		Rr both red	
parents	Rr		Rr
gametes	R or r		R or r
second generation (F_2)		rR	
		RR rr Rr	3 red 1 white

💡 *If you have to choose letters to represent dominant and recessive characteristics, make sure you choose letters that are noticeably different, i.e. 'R' and 'r', not 'S' and 's'*

Variation

Some human and animal characteristics are controlled by genes and so are inherited, for example eye colour and blood group. The environment controls other characteristics, for example scars or language. Some characteristics are a combination of both, for example intelligence, body mass or height. This is illustrated by

identical twins that possess identical genes but may follow different diets. The same is true for plants: they inherit certain features but are more influenced by environmental factors, such as lack of sunlight or minerals.

A worked example – inheritance of eye colour

Remember, we have two alleles for eye colour – one from each parent – making up a gene.

- The allele for brown eyes is **dominant**, so it can be represented by the letter 'B'.

- The allele for blue eyes is **recessive**, so it is represented by the letter 'b'.

- If the mother and father are both **heterozygous** for eye colour, they have the genotype 'Bb'.

What colour eyes will the children of heterozygous parents have?

We can show the possible outcomes using a **Punnett square**.

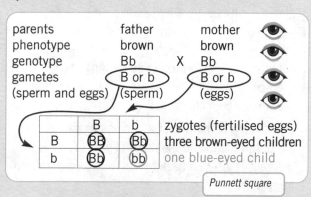

Punnett square

This gives a 3 : 1 ratio of brown to blue eyes.

Different combinations of genotypes can be crossed and the outcomes worked out in the same way using a Punnett square. For example; what would happen if the mother was **heterozygous** for eye colour (Bb) and the father was **homozygous** for blue eyes (bb)?

This gives a 1 : 1 ratio of brown eyes to blue eyes.

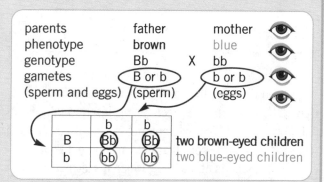

Remember, the ratios are only probabilities and may not always happen.

Genetics questions are a good way to gain marks, as long as you show all your working and label everything as you go along.

Definitions

Recessive means it is the weaker allele and only has an effect in the homozygous recessive condition.

Dominant means it is the stronger allele and has an effect in the heterozygous condition.

The **genotype** is the type of alleles an organism carries: i.e. the genotype of the red pea plants could be RR or Rr. Although the genotypes are different, the plants are both red because red is dominant.

The **phenotype** is what an organism physically looks like, the result of what genotype the organism has.

If an organism has both alleles the same, it is **homozygous dominant** (RR) or **homozygous recessive** (rr).

If an organism has different alleles, it is **heterozygous** (Rr).

QUICK TEST

1. Is a plant with a genotype RR homozygous or heterozygous dominant?

2. Does a person with blue eyes have a genotype or phenotype bb?

3. Is a plant that has two different alleles heterozygous or homozygous?

4. What does recessive mean?

5. What does dominant mean?

6. What is a zygote?

7. What are gametes?

8. What does monohybrid inheritance mean?

9. Predict the outcome of a cross between two blue-eyed homozygous recessive parents.

10. What would be the genotype of a brown-eyed child if brown was the dominant characteristic? (B = brown, b = blue)

Genetic engineering

Genetic engineering is the process by which genes from one organism are removed and inserted into the cells of another. It has many exciting possibilities, but is not without its problems. Scientists can now genetically modify plants and animals using the process of genetic engineering.

Gene therapy

It may be possible to use genetic engineering to treat inherited diseases such as **cystic fibrosis**. Sufferers could be cured if the correct gene is inserted into their body cells. The problem that exists with cystic fibrosis is that the cells that need the correct gene are in many parts of the body, which makes it difficult to remove them to insert the required gene. Another problem is that even if the correct gene is inserted into the body cells, the cells would not multiply. This means that there would be many cells that still have the faulty gene.

Manipulating genes

You have seen how our genes code for a particular protein that enables all our normal life processes to function. **Many diseases are caused when the body cannot make a particular protein**.

Genetic engineering has been used to treat diabetic people through the production of the protein, insulin. The gene that codes for insulin can be found in human pancreas cells. The insulin gene is selected, isolated and inserted into the bacteria. The bacteria replicate, making insulin.

Risks of genetic engineering

Manipulating bacteria for use in producing proteins might result in previously harmless bacteria mutating into disease-causing bacteria. Gene therapy is potentially a way forward in curing fatal diseases, but it poses risks as inserting genes into human cells may make them cancerous.

There is a possibility that a human egg can be taken out of the womb and the harmful genes removed, before it is inserted back to continue its growth into a human.

Genetic engineering is seen by many as manipulating the 'stuff of life': is it morally and ethically wrong to interfere with nature? There is still a lot of unease about the methods used as nobody can be completely sure what the results will be.

> *You may be asked to provide arguments for and against the use of genetic engineering, so be prepared to discuss the benefits and risks involved.*

Other human proteins made in this way include the human-growth hormone that is used to treat children who do not grow properly.

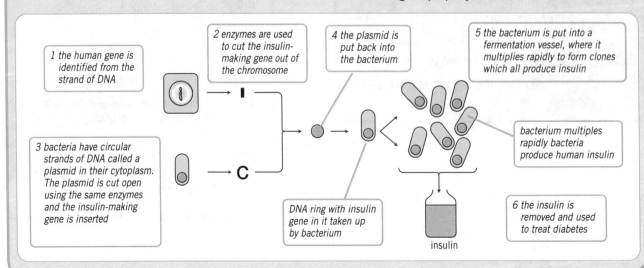

1 the human gene is identified from the strand of DNA

2 enzymes are used to cut the insulin-making gene out of the chromosome

3 bacteria have circular strands of DNA called a plasmid in their cytoplasm. The plasmid is cut open using the same enzymes and the insulin-making gene is inserted

4 the plasmid is put back into the bacterium

5 the bacterium is put into a fermentation vessel, where it multiplies rapidly to form clones which all produce insulin

DNA ring with insulin gene in it taken up by bacterium

bacterium multiples rapidly bacteria produce human insulin

6 the insulin is removed and used to treat diabetes

insulin

The benefits of genetic engineering

Genetic engineering benefits industry, medicine and agriculture in many ways. We have developed plants that are resistant to pests and diseases and plants that can grow in adverse environmental conditions. Wheat and other crops have been developed that can take nitrogen from the air directly and produce proteins without the need for costly fertilisers. Tomatoes and other sorts of fruit are now able to stay fresher for longer. Animals are engineered to produce chemicals in their milk, such as drugs and human antibodies. The list seems endless and there are no doubts as to the benefits of genetic engineering now and in the

Tomatoes can be genetically engineered to stay fresh longer by inserting a gene from fish into their cells. Would you eat one?

future, but there are also risks and moral issues that are associated with this relatively modern technology.

Human genome project

This project was completed in 2003. It aimed to identify all the genes in human DNA and study them. The benefits included an improved diagnosis of disease and earlier detection of genetic diseases in families, such as breast cancer and Alzheimer's.

The use of DNA in forensic science has improved greatly.

It is now possible to identify suspects, clear the wrongly accused, identify paternity, and match organ donors with recipients. A person's 'DNA fingerprint' is unique. There is an extremely slim chance of another person having the same 'fingerprint'. Scientists identify a region of DNA that is unique to that person and can then build up a profile.

Transgenic animals and designer babies

The term 'designer baby' refers to the use of the pre-implantation diagnosis of embryos for disease or sex using the IVF technique. Healthy embryos are then implanted in the womb for growth.

At present in the UK, it is illegal to pre-determine the sex of a baby unless it is linked to a genetic disease. Some people wish to have a baby with the right genetic make-up in order to cure a child they already have. This is under strict discussion and approval, and is dealt with on a case-to-case basis. Many people believe

this is interfering with nature and is not, therefore, morally acceptable. In the future it may be possible to 'cure' diseases by replacing faulty sections of DNA. This is called germ line therapy. It may also be possible to create 'designer babies' with specific features and intelligence. But is this ethical?

A transgenic animal is one that carries a foreign gene that has been deliberately inserted, for example a cow that produces milk that is low in cholesterol and contains human antibodies.

 Give an example of a transgenic animal and what it is used for.

 What are genes made of?

 Give an example of the use of bacteria to treat a disease.

 What are the risks associated with using bacteria to produce human proteins?

⑤ What is gene therapy?

Inherited diseases

Not all diseases are caused by pathogens. Genes pass on characteristics from one generation to the next. Sometimes 'faulty' genes are inherited that cause diseases.

Inherited diseases are called *genetic diseases*.

Genetic screening

Genetic testing is now possible to determine whether adults have a genetic disease. The technique is not yet legal for employers and insurance companies, but do you think it should be? Adults could be screened and then decide whether to have children or not.

Foetuses can be tested using pre-implantation diagnosis, but if a genetic disease is discovered then the couple have to make a decision as to whether to continue with the pregnancy or terminate it.

Symptoms
The brain degenerates and the sufferer has uncontrolled, jerky movements. The sufferer becomes moody and depressed and their memory is affected.

Treatment
There is no cure. Onset of the disease is late: the sufferer is about 30–40 years old before they realise that they have it. Consequently many have already had children and passed on the disease.

Huntington's chorea

Causes
Huntington's chorea is caused by a **dominant allele (H)**. This means only one allele is needed to pass on the disease. As a result, **all heterozygous people are sufferers (Hh)**. The only people free from the disease are **homozygous recessive (hh)**. It affects one in 20 000 people, so is a rare disease. There is a 50% chance of inheriting the disease if just one parent is a carrier.

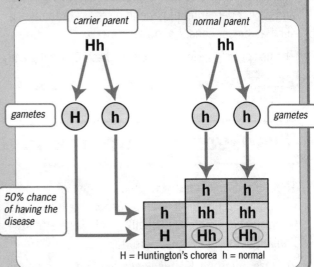

H = Huntington's chorea   h = normal

Cystic fibrosis 1

Causes

Cystic fibrosis is the most common inherited disease in Britain: about one in 2000 children born in Britain has cystic fibrosis. It is caused by a **recessive allele (c)**, carried by about one person in 20. This makes the chances of two carriers marrying, one in 400. People who are **heterozygous** with the genotype (Cc) are said to be **carriers**. They have no ill effects. Only people who are **homozygous** for this allele (cc) are affected.

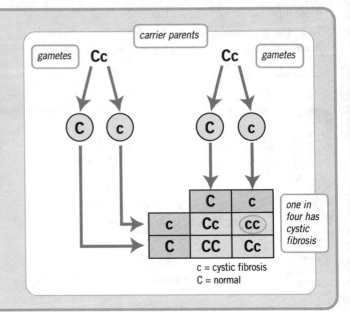

c = cystic fibrosis
C = normal

Cystic fibrosis 2

Symptoms

Cystic fibrosis sufferers produce large amounts of **thick, sticky mucus** that can block air passages and digestive tubes. The child has difficulty breathing and absorbing food.

The mucus slows down the exchange of oxygen and carbon dioxide between the lungs and blood. The mucus also **encourages bacteria to grow**, which cause chest infections.

Treatment

There is still no cure: treatment involves **physiotherapy** to try to remove some of the mucus and **strong** **antibiotics** to treat the infections. It was only in 1989 that the gene that causes cystic fibrosis was discovered. This allowed a test to be developed, which can tell if a person is a carrier by analysing their DNA. If a couple know that they are carriers they have a difficult decision to make. A **genetic counsellor** can explain to them that there is a one in four chance of having a child with cystic fibrosis. They then have to decide if the risk of having children is too great.

> Don't rush through the genetic diagrams as you may be asked to draw them in the exam.

Stem cell therapy

Stem cell therapy is on going research in the treatment of human disease and organ failure. Stem cells are cells that have yet to specialise into different types of tissue. They are found in adult bone marrow, human embryos and the umbilical cord. Adult stem cells do not have the same potential as embryonic stem cells to treat illness. Stem cells have the ability to divide and specialise into any tissue needed, such as nerve cell tissue.

Stem cell therapy research and use is still in the early stages. It requires much more funding, support and regulation, particularly when the stem cells involved are from donated human embryos. There is an ethical dilemma concerning the moral and legal status of these embryos.

Some plant cells behave differently to animal cells, and like stemcells, they can continue to grow throughout life. Animal cells lose this ability when they mature. They only divide to repair and replace once maximum growth is reached. This is demonstrated when cuttings are taken from plants. Cuttings are simply sections of a plant, and yet are capable, under the right conditions, of growing into an identical plant.

Scientific processes

The potential for stem cell therapy is endless. Stem cells can be used to replace tissue that has lost its function, e.g. in heart problems. They can also be used to treat genetic diseases by being implanted into the donor before the genetic disease has developed. This technique has achieved some success when treating brain disease.

QUICK TEST

1. How is cystic fibrosis inherited?
2. What are the symptoms of cystic fibrosis?
3. How is cystic fibrosis treated?
4. What are the chances of two carrier parents having a child who suffers from cystic fibrosis?
5. What is a stem cell?
6. Where are stem cells found?
7. How can we potentially use stem cell therapy?
8. What are the symptoms of Huntington's chorea?
9. Why are the chances of inheriting Huntington's chorea so high if just one parent is a carrier?

Selective breeding

People are always trying to breed animals and plants with special characteristics. For example, a fast racehorse or a cow that produces lots of milk.

Selective breeding is a technique used by humans to produce desired characteristics in animals and plants, it is also known as artificial selection.

Artificial selection

The procedures involved in artificial selection are as follows:

■ Select the individuals with the best characteristics.

■ Breed them together using sexual reproduction.

■ Hopefully, some of the offspring will have inherited some of the desirable features: the best offspring are selected and then bred together.

■ This is repeated over generations until the offspring have all the desired characteristics.

Selective breeding in animals

The farm pig has been selectively bred over the years from a wild pig.

The features that have been bred in are:

■ less hair   ■ a quieter temperament   ■ fatter.

Can you think why? Other animals are also selectively bred.

■ Cows have been selectively bred to produce a greater quantity of milk.

■ Beef cattle have been bred to produce better meat.

The problem with only breeding from the best cows and bulls is that the cows can only give birth once a year. New techniques have therefore been developed.

wild pig

modern farm pig

Embryo transfer

The process is as follows:

■ Sperm is taken from the best bull.

■ The best cow is given hormones to stimulate the production of lots of eggs.

■ The eggs are removed from the cow and are fertilised in a petri dish.

■ The embryos are allowed to develop, but are then split apart to form clones before they become specialised.

■ The embryos are then implanted into other cows called surrogates, where they grow into offspring.

The advantage is that the sperm and the eggs can be frozen to be used at a later date and a large number of offspring can be produced from one bull and one cow.

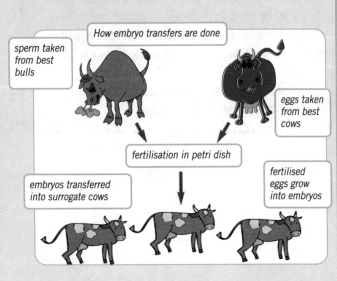

How embryo transfers are done

sperm taken from best bulls

eggs taken from best cows

fertilisation in petri dish

fertilised eggs grow into embryos

embryos transferred into surrogate cows

Selective breeding in plants

Selectively bred individuals may not always produce the desired characteristics as **sexual reproduction always produces variation**. With plants, this can be overcome by producing **clones**. **Clones are genetically identical individuals**. To produce clones, asexual reproduction is needed. Many plants reproduce asexually on their own, for example strawberry plants which produce runners.

Problems with selective breeding

The problem is a **reduction in the number of alleles in a population**. If animals or plants are continually bred from the same best animals or plants, the animals and plants will all be very similar. If there is a change in the environment, the new animals and plants may not be able to cope with it. There may be no alleles left to breed new varieties of plants and animals selectively. It is important to keep wild varieties alive, to maintain species variation.

 Learn the four steps involved in selective breeding and remember it is also called artificial selection.

Tissue culture and cuttings

Gardeners can produce new, identical plants by **taking cuttings** from an original parent plant. The plants are dipped in rooting powder containing hormones and are kept in a damp atmosphere to grow into new plants. The new plants would be clones.

Tissue culture is a technique used by commercial plant breeders. They take just a few plant cells and grow a new plant from them, using a special growth medium containing hormones. The advantages are that new plants can be grown quickly and cheaply all year round,

> From cuttings to clones
>
> *trim off lower leaves and make a slanting cut just below a leaf stalk*
>
> *roots grow from stem after several weeks in water and hormone powder*

with special properties such as resistance to diseases. Plants also reproduce sexually, attracting insects for pollination. The resulting plants show **variation**.

This is very important because if they only produced clones and a new disease developed, it would kill the one clone and all the others in that species as they would be all the same.

Dolly the sheep

Dolly the sheep was the first mammal cloned in 1996. She died prematurely in 2003. Her early death fuelled the debate about the long-term health problems of clones. The procedure to create her was as follows:

■ The nucleus was removed from an egg cell.

■ The egg cell nucleus was replaced with the nucleus of an udder cell.
■ This cell was then implanted into another sheep.
■ The cell then grew into a clone of the sheep from which the udder cell came.

Scientific processes

The implications of cloning Dolly the sheep are that scientists are looking at ways of using genetically engineered animals to grow replacement organs for humans. This poses many ethical concerns, not least the problems of rejection of the organ by the recipient (tissue rejection). What do you think?

> *Make sure you can list the advantages of selective breeding and also the disadvantages.*

QUICK TEST

1. What is selective breeding?
2. What is the difference between artificial selection and natural selection?
3. What are clones?
4. Name two techniques used in the selective breeding of animals, particularly cows and bulls.
5. Name two methods of selective breeding in plants.

Pyramids

Before looking at pyramids, you need to recall that a food chain shows us simply who eats who and a food web is a series of linked food chains that gives us a more realistic picture. Energy enters food chains when plants absorb sunlight during photosynthesis. Plants are known as autotrophs or producers, as they produce all their own organic compounds from carbon dioxide and the sun. Animals are called heterotrophs or consumers as they depend on plants for their energy and raw materials.

Pyramids of numbers

A food chain tells us, simply, who eats who. A pyramid of numbers tells us how many organisms are involved at each stage in the food chain. At each level of the food chain (trophic level) the number of organisms is generally reduced.

| fox |
| rabbit |
| grass |

Sometimes a pyramid of numbers does not look like a pyramid at all as it doesn't take into account the **size** of the organisms.

A rose bush counts as one organism, but a rose bush can support many herbivores.

| blackbird |
| ladybirds |
| aphids |
| rose bush |

In this pyramid of numbers, the top carnivores are fleas that feed on single fox.

| fleas |
| fox |
| rabbits |
| lettuce |

Pyramids of biomass

A biomass pyramid takes into account **the size or mass of an organism** at each level. If we take the information from the pyramid of numbers and multiply it by the organism's mass then we get a pyramid shape again.

A single rose bush weighs more than the aphids, and lots of aphids weigh more than the few ladybirds that feed on them. A blackbird weighs less than the many ladybirds it feeds on.

| blackbird |
| ladybirds |
| aphids |
| rose bush |

A biomass pyramid takes account of the mass of each organism

Even though there are a lot of fleas, they weigh less than the fox they feed on.

The fox weighs less than the number of rabbits it

| fleas |
| fox |
| rabbits |
| lettuce |

eats, and the number of lettuces the rabbits eat weigh more than the rabbits.

> *Questions in the exam may provide you with actual numbers or masses of the organisms involved in food chains. Make sure you draw them to scale.*

Loss of energy in food chains 1

Food chains rarely have more than four or five links in them. This is because **energy is lost along the way**. The final organism is only getting a fraction of the energy that was produced at the beginning of the food chain.

Plants absorb energy from the sun. Only a small fraction of this energy is converted into glucose during photosynthesis. Some energy is lost to decomposers as plants shed their leaves, seeds or fruit. The plant uses some energy during respiration and growth.

The plant's biomass increases, which provides food for the herbivores. Only approximately **10% of the original energy from the sun** is passed on to the primary consumer in the plant's biomass. The primary consumer also has energy losses and only **approximately 10% of its total energy intake is passed on to the secondary consumer.**

> *There is always competition for resources in a food web, try to imagine the effect that a change in one organism's numbers will have on the rest of the food web.*

Loss of energy in food chains 2

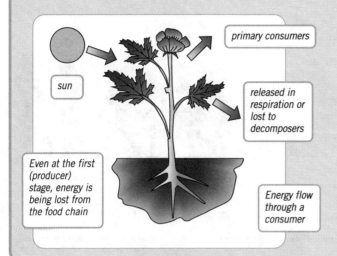

sun

primary consumers

released in respiration or lost to decomposers

Even at the first (producer) stage, energy is being lost from the food chain

Energy flow through a consumer

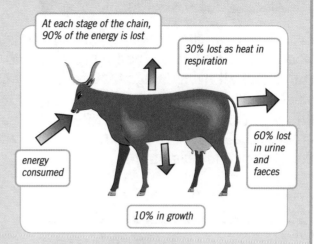

At each stage of the chain, 90% of the energy is lost

30% lost as heat in respiration

energy consumed

60% lost in urine and faeces

10% in growth

Where does the energy go?

The 90% energy loss at each stage goes on life processes such as **respiration**. Respiration **releases heat energy** to the surroundings. Animals that are warm-blooded use up a lot of energy in **keeping warm** and so

they need to eat a lot more food.

As you can see from the diagram above of energy transfers in the cow, a lot of energy is lost in **urine** and **faeces**. Also, **not all of the organism's body mass is eaten**.

Efficiency of food production

As so much energy is lost along food chains, we must look at ways to improve the efficiency of food production and reduce losses. There are two ways this can be done:

1 **Reduce the number of stages in the food chain**. It is more energy efficient to eat plant produce than meat.

2 **Rear animals intensively**. If you restrict their movement and keep them warm, the animals won't need feeding as much.

However, the second method is not considered a decent way to keep animals.

> ⓘ *A common exam question is about the energy losses in food chains and how to reduce them, so make sure you learn them thoroughly.*

1 Why do food chains only have four or five links?

2 What do pyramids of numbers show?

3 What don't they take into account?

4 What pyramids can be drawn using the mass of animals and plants?

5 Where does a plant get its original energy source?

6 Approximately how much energy is passed on from the producer to the consumer?

7 Why do warm-blooded animals need to eat a lot of food?

8 In animals, where does most of the energy go?

9 List the ways that energy is lost in food chains.

10 How can we reduce energy loss in food chains?

Evolution

Evolution is all about change and improvement from simple life forms. The *theory of evolution* states that all living things that exist today or existed, evolved from simple life forms three billion years ago. *Natural selection* is the process that causes evolution. *Fossils* provide the evidence for evolution.

The theory of evolution – from animal to human

The theory of evolution

organisms produce a large number of offspring

in any species there is a variation between individuals

Natural selection, as demonstrated in the wild

there is a struggle for existence

organisms with useful characteristics are more likely to survive and pass them on to the next generation

Religious theories are based on the need for a 'creator' for all life to exist on Earth, but there are other theories.

Charles Darwin, a British naturalist, first put forward his theory about 140 years ago.

Darwin visited the Galapagos Islands off the coast of South America and made a number of observations that led to his theory of evolution.

1 Organisms produce more offspring than can possibly survive.

2 Population numbers remain fairly constant despite this.

3 All organisms in a species show variation.

4 Some of these variations are inherited.

He also concluded from these observations that, since there were more offspring produced than could survive, there must be a struggle for existence. This led to the strongest and fittest offspring surviving and passing on their genes to their offspring.

This is sometimes called the **survival of the fittest** or **natural selection**.

Natural selection

Darwin stated that the process of natural selection was the basis for evolution. A species is defined as a group of living things that are able to breed together and produce fertile offspring. Within a species there is variation between individuals. Changes in the environment may affect some individuals and not others. **Only those who can adapt to suit their new environment survive to breed and pass on their advantageous genes.**

Other factors that tend to prevent all offspring surviving are competition for food, predators and disease. Eventually, nature decides which individuals should survive and breed. There is a **'survival of the fittest'**. The combined effects of natural selection, selective breeding, genetic engineering and mutations may lead to a new species forming.

Natural selection in action

An example of the environment causing changes in a species is that of the **peppered moth**. Peppered moths live in woodlands on lichen-covered trees. There are two types of peppered moth: a light-coloured speckled form and a dark form. The dark-coloured moth was caused by a mutation and was usually eaten by predators. In the 1850s, the dark type of moth was rare, but pollution from factories started to blacken tree trunks. The dark moth was then at an advantage because it was camouflaged. In 1895, most of the population of moths were dark. In cleaner, less polluted areas, the light-coloured moth had an advantage against predators and so it still survived to breed.

 dark-coloured moth against a soot-covered tree

 the pale moth is at a disadvantage in polluted areas

Pollution played a key role in the 'survival of the fittest' for these peppered moths

Extinction

Species that are unable to adapt to their surroundings become extinct. Examples include the mammoth, the dodo, and the sabretoothed tiger. Extinction can also be caused by changes in the environment, new predators, new disease, new competition or human activity, e.g. hunting, pollution or habitat destruction.

Fossils

Fossils are the remains of dead organisms that lived millions of years ago. They are found in rocks. Most dead organisms decay and disintegrate but the following are ways that fossils can be formed:

1 The hard parts of animals that don't decay form into a rock.

2 Minerals that preserve their shape, gradually replace the softer parts of animals that decay very slowly.

3 Fossils are formed in areas where one or more of the conditions needed for decay are absent, for example in areas where there is no **oxygen, moisture or warmth**.

Fossils provide evidence for evolution. They are preserved in rock. Generally, the younger fossils are found nearer the surface.

The evolution of the horse is clearly shown by fossils. Look at the changes in their size and feet caused by the changes in the environment over the years. Natural selection has operated to produce the modern horse.

The modern horse: an example of natural selection

60 million years ago — marshy land

40 million years ago

30 million years ago — splayed out digits to prevent sinking in mud

10 million years ago

1 million years ago — single hoof foot — harder ground

⚠ *The peppered moth and the evolution of the horse are popular examples to demonstrate evolution by natural selection.*

Scientific processes

Darwin's theory became widely accepted eventually, but a man called Lamarck suggested that animals evolved features according to how much they used them. Giraffes, for example, grew longer necks because they needed to reach food.

QUICK TEST

① Who were the two scientists that put forward their theories of evolution?

② Whose theory was gradually accepted?

③ What prevents all the organisms in a species surviving?

④ Which individuals would survive a change in the environment?

⑤ What process causes evolution?

⑥ Why did the feet of the modern horse change?

⑦ Which type of peppered moth would survive in industrial regions and why?

Adaptation and competition

- A *habitat* is where an organism lives: it provides the conditions needed for that organism to survive.
- A *community* consists of living things in the *habitat*.
- Each *community* is made up of different populations of animals and plants.
- Each *population* is adapted to live in that particular *habitat*.

Sizes of populations

Population numbers cannot keep growing out of control: factors that keep the population from becoming too large are called **limiting factors**. The factors that affect the size of a population are:

- the amount of food and water available
- predators or grazing – who may eat the animal or plant
- disease
- climate, temperature, floods, droughts and storms
- competition for space, mates, light, food and water
- human activity such as pollution or destruction of habitats.

Predator and prey graphs

In a community, the number of animals stays fairly constant. This is partly due to the amount of food limiting the size of the populations. A **predator** is an animal that hunts and kills another animal. The **prey** is the hunted animal.

Populations of predator and prey go in cycles.

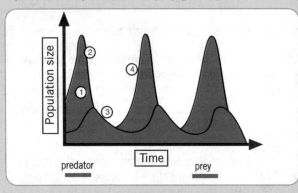

predator   Time   prey

1 If the population of prey increases, there is more food for the predator, so its numbers increase.
2 This causes the number of prey to decrease as they are eaten.
3 This, in turn, causes the number of predators to decrease, as there is not enough food to support the increased numbers of predators and they must compete with one another for food.
4 If the predator numbers fall, the prey numbers can increase again, as they are no longer being eaten, and so on.

Predators have adapted to survive by being strong, agile and fast. They have good vision and a camouflaged body. They also tend to hunt in packs, have a variety of prey, and often hunt the young, sick and old.

Prey have also adapted to survive. The best adapted prey escape and breed. Adaptations of prey include being able to run, swim and fly fast, living in large groups, having a horrible taste when eaten, and exhibiting warning colours or a camouflaged body.

predator

prey

Competition

As populations grow, there may be overcrowding and limited resources to support the growing numbers. Animals have to compete for **space, food and water** in their struggle to survive. Only the strongest will live, leading to the survival of the fittest. Even plants compete for **space, light, water and nutrients**.

Adaptations of animals

You never see a polar bear in the desert or a camel at the North Pole. This is because they have not **adapted** to live there. They have adapted to live where they do: they have **special features** that help them survive.

A polar bear lives in cold, arctic regions of the world. It has many features that enable it to survive.

The polar bear: adapted to deal with arctic conditions

- It has a **thick coat** to keep in body heat, as well as a **layer of blubber** for insulation.
- Its coat is **white** so that it can blend into its surroundings.
- Its **fur is greasy** so that it doesn't hold water after swimming. This prevents cooling by evaporation.
- A polar bear has **big feet** to spread its weight on snow and ice; it also has big, **sharp claws** to catch fish.
- It is a **good swimmer** and **runner** in order to catch prey.

- The shape of a polar bear is **compact** even though it is large. This keeps its surface area to a minimum to reduce loss of body heat.

A camel has features that enable it to survive in the hot deserts of the world.

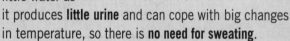

The camel: ideally suited to living in hot, dry deserts

- The camel has an ability to **drink** a lot of water and **store** it.
- It loses very little water as it produces **little urine** and can cope with big changes in temperature, so there is **no need for sweating**.
- All its fat is stored in the humps, so there is **no insulation layer**.
- Its **sandy** colour provides **camouflage**.
- It has a **large surface area** to enable it to lose heat effectively.

> *The adaptations of a camel and polar bear are popular examples for the exam but be aware that there are many more animals and plants that show adaptions to their own environment.*

Adaptations of plants

The cactus has adapted to live in hot, dry conditions. Its rounded shape helps to combat water losses (by reducing the surface area to volume ratio), as does its thick cuticles and leaves reduced to spines. The cactus is also capable of storing water and has long roots to reach water deep beneath the surface of the ground.

Plants have adapted according to pollination methods. The flowers of wind-pollinated plants have light, feathery stigmas that tend to be exposed and small, light grains of pollen. Insect-pollinated plants have colourful scented petals to attract insects, sticky pollen and sweet nectar.

QUICK TEST

1. What is a habitat?
2. Define the word community.
3. What makes up a population?
4. What things do animals compete for?
5. What things do plants compete for?
6. If the number of prey increases, what will happen to the number of predators?
7. Why do the numbers of prey and predators in a community stay fairly constant?
8. How does the polar bear's coat help it survive in the Arctic?
9. How does the camel's large surface area help it survive in the desert?
10. What factor determines whether animals or plants survive in their environment?

Environmental damage 1

Improvements in agriculture, health and medicine have meant a dramatic *rise in human populations*. An increase in population size leads to an increase in pollution and higher demands on the world's resources.

Effects on the environment

Humans are using up the Earth's resources, including fossil fuels, at an alarming rate.

Burning fossil fuels contributes to **acid rain** and the **greenhouse effect** by releasing harmful gases into the air.

Gases such as sulphur dioxide dissolve in rain and make it acidic. Acid rain damages wildlife and pollutes rivers and lakes. Carbon dioxide is also released into the atmosphere by burning fossil fuels. This gas traps heat inside the Earth's atmosphere and causes the temperature of the Earth to increase. This is known as the greenhouse effect.

Fertilisers

Plants need nutrients to grow, which they take up from the soil. With intensive farming methods, nutrients are quickly used up, so the farmer has to replace them with artificial fertilisers. Fertilisers enable farmers to produce more crops in a smaller area of land and can reduce the need to destroy the countryside for extra space. Problems, however, particularly in the form of **eutrophication**, are caused by the use of fertilisers.

Eutrophication

If too much fertiliser is added to the soil and it rains soon afterwards, the fertiliser finds its way into rivers and lakes. This causes the water plants to grow more quickly and cover the surface of the water. More water plants means more competition for light. Inevitably, some plants die. Microbes (bacteria and fungi) break down the dead plants and use up oxygen for respiration. This reduces the amount of oxygen available for animals and so they die of suffocation. **Untreated sewage** pumped into rivers and streams also causes eutrophication.

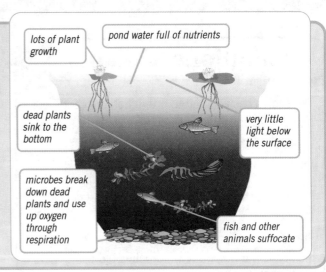

lots of plant growth

pond water full of nutrients

dead plants sink to the bottom

very little light below the surface

microbes break down dead plants and use up oxygen through respiration

fish and other animals suffocate

Deforestation

In the UK, there are not many forests left. In under-developed countries, people are chopping down trees to provide timber or space for agriculture, to try to provide for the growing numbers of people. This causes several problems to the environment. Burning this timber **increases the level of carbon dioxide** in the air. Forests absorb carbon dioxide in the air and provide us with oxygen. Chopping down trees leads to **soil erosion** as the soil is exposed to rain and wind. The trees evaporate water into the air and without them there will be a **decrease in rainfall**. Destroying forests also **destroys many different animal and plant habitats**.

Intensive farming

Farming has had to become more intensive to try and provide more food from a given area of land. Intensive farming can produce more food, but it has its problems. Many people regard the intensive farming of animals (such as fish farming and battery farming) as cruel. In order to produce more food from the land, **fertilisers and pesticides** are needed.

Hydroponics is the growth of plants without soil in a special medium such as peat. The plants need support and carefully controlled mineral levels, fertilisers are often used.

Learn arguments for and against intensive farming.

Destruction of the land

An increase in industry has led to the need to take over the land, which destroys wildlife and causes pollution.

we use land for building

dumping our rubbish

getting raw materials

farming to feed the world

Pesticides

Pesticides are used to kill the insects that damage crops. They also kill harmless insects, which can cause a shortage of food for insect-eating birds.
There is always the danger that pesticides can get washed into rivers and lakes and **end up in our food chains**. This was the case in the 1960s, when a pesticide called DDT got into the food chain and threatened populations of animals.

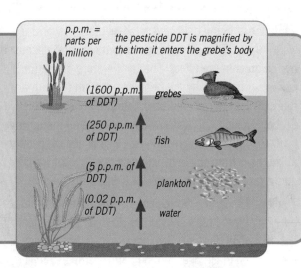
p.p.m. = parts per million

the pesticide DDT is magnified by the time it enters the grebe's body

(1600 p.p.m. of DDT) grebes

(250 p.p.m. of DDT) fish

(5 p.p.m. of DDT) plankton

(0.02 p.p.m. of DDT) water

What can be done?

A possible solution to some of the problems is **organic farming**. Organic farming produces less food per area of land and can be expensive, but it attempts to leave the countryside as it is and is kinder to animals.

Organic farming uses **manure as a fertiliser, sets aside land** to allow wild plants and animals to flourish and uses **biological control of pests**. Biological control of pests is the use of other animals to eat pests. It is not as effective but produces no harmful effects.

QUICK TEST

 What problems can the use of pesticides cause?

 What is deforestation?

 How does deforestation contribute to the greenhouse effect?

 What other problems does deforestation cause?

What could be used as an alternative to fertilisers?

Environmental damage 2

Our Earth is in danger because of the harmful effects of pollutants on air, water and land. Humans are responsible for the destruction of our planet and unless we do something about it, serious harm will come to the Earth and all who live here.

Pollution

A pollutant is a substance that harms living things – animals, plants or humans. Pollutants can spread through the air, water and soil.

The greenhouse effect

Evidence is being collected to show that the world is warming up. This is called **global warming** and is caused by the **greenhouse effect**. The temperature of the Earth is kept in balance by the heat we get from the sun and the heat that is radiated back into the atmosphere. Carbon dioxide and water vapour act like an insulating layer (like glass in a greenhouse) to **trap and keep** some of the heat from the sun. This is **natural global warming** and it provides enough heat for living things.

The levels of carbon dioxide are increasing because of the burning of fossil fuels and cutting down of trees (which absorb carbon dioxide). This increase in carbon dioxide is trapping too much heat and the Earth's temperature is slowly rising above normal levels.

Methane gas is also contributing to the greenhouse effect. Methane is produced naturally from cattle waste and rice fields.

Problems caused by the greenhouse effect
Changes in temperature could cause **melting of the polar ice caps**, which in turn would cause **raised sea levels**. Serious **flooding** could result. Plants may be killed by the warming and weeds may thrive as they grow well on extra carbon dioxide.

Acid rain

Burning fossil fuels is the main cause of acid rain. Cars and power stations are the main culprits. The gases **sulphur dioxide** and **various nitrogen oxides** are released by the burning of fuel. They dissolve in water vapour in the clouds and fall as **acid rain**. Acid rain kills fish and trees, and damages buildings.

What can be done?
■ We can look for **alternative energy sources**.
■ We can use unleaded petrol and reduce the need for cars.
■ We can **use catalytic converters** in cars to reduce emissions of harmful gases.
■ We can **stop large scale deforestation** because trees absorb carbon dioxide.

💡 *The effects of acid rain and the greenhouse effect are common exam questions.*

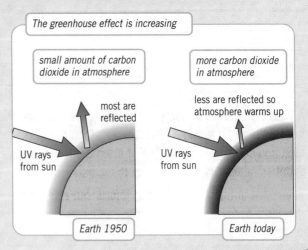

The greenhouse effect is increasing

small amount of carbon dioxide in atmosphere

more carbon dioxide in atmosphere

most are reflected

less are reflected so atmosphere warms up

UV rays from sun

UV rays from sun

Earth 1950

Earth today

Pollution of the soil and water

Fertilisers and pesticides used on land can be washed into rivers and seas, causing damage to wildlife. Farm waste can have the same effects on wildlife. Factory waste and sewage are often dumped at sea. Oil spillages at sea are also a problem for marine life and seabirds and can also ruin beaches.

Pollution of the air

Factories and cars use fossil fuels. They release **carbon dioxide** (which contributes to the greenhouse effect), **sulphur dioxide** and nitrogen oxides (which cause acid rain). Smoke from burning contains particles of soot (**carbon**), which can blacken buildings and collect on plants, preventing them from photosynthesising. The smoke from car engines also contains lead, which is known to cause damage to the nervous system if inhaled.

CFCs (chlorofluorocarbons) are used in aerosols, refrigerators and in plastic foam. CFCs are also contributing to the greenhouse effect by causing the ozone layer to develop holes. This means that harmful UV rays are now reaching the Earth's surface, which can lead to increased risk of skin cancer. Other gases are now being used instead of CFCs but the harmful effects of the CFCs already released will continue for some time.

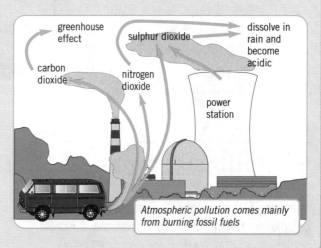

Atmospheric pollution comes mainly from burning fossil fuels

Water resources

In the UK, our water comes from rainwater, underground water, rivers and the sea. All water must be purified before use, as it contains bacteria, suspended particles, floating objects and pollutants. The water is filtered to remove larger objects and then the sediment settles on the bottom where it is removed. The water is also chlorinated to remove bacteria.

Water is an important resource that must be conserved and kept clean, particularly in developing countries where water can spread many diseases and medication is scarce. There are animals and plants called **indicator species** that, in their absence or presence, indicate pollution. For example, the sludge worm and water louse are present in polluted water. Similarly, certain species of algae and lichen grow in areas of high air pollution.

Conservation and sustainable development

With the human population increasing and using up resources, we need to find a way of maintaining our quality of life for future generations. This is known as sustainable development.

It is important to protect our food supply, maintain biodiversity and conserve resources as we do not know what the future may hold. Many species of animals have already become extinct and many more are in danger of extinction, such as the red squirrel, osprey and whale. We need to look at ways of protecting habitats, breeding in captivity to increase numbers and giving endangered species legal protection.

An effective way of maintaining fish stocks and our woodlands is to introduce quotas and replant woodland. Sustainable development requires a lot of planning and co-operation at every level if our valuable resources are not to run out and many more species become extinct.

QUICK TEST

1. What is the main cause of atmospheric pollution?
2. What gases cause acid rain?
3. What damage does acid rain cause?
4. Why is the Earth warming up?
5. How can we reduce acid rain? Give two examples.
6. What causes holes in the ozone layer?
7. What harmful chemical in car exhausts damages the nervous system?

Ecology and classification

We are surrounded by a huge variety of living organisms in a variety of habitats. Ecology is the study of living things in their habitats. In any one habitat, the numbers of organisms are usually large, so we use sampling techniques to get an idea of who lives there and to estimate the population size. Different types of keys can be used to identify animals and plants.

Sampling techniques

There are a variety of techniques used to sample organisms in their habitats. For example: quadrats, pooters and pitfalls, which are described below.

Quadrats

A quadrat is a wooden or metal frame, usually 1 m² in area. The quadrat is placed randomly, for example in a field, and the number of plants belonging to a given species is counted within the quadrat. If the process is carried out 10 times, we can estimate the number of plants belonging to that species in the field.

Example method

- Add up the number of daisies in 10 quadrats, e.g. 30.
- Divide by 10 to find the average per quadrat, e.g. 0.3.
- Work out the total area of the field, e.g. 500 m x 500 m x 250 000 m²
- If one square metre quadrat has three daisies in it, then the whole field will have 3 x 250 000 x 750 000 daisies.
- Remember, this is only an estimate but is better than counting each and every daisy!

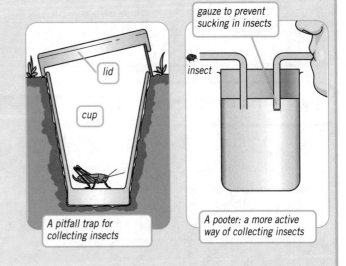

A pitfall trap for collecting insects

A pooter: a more active way of collecting insects

and identify them; and pitfall traps can be used to get an idea of the number of animals in a habitat.

> To get the bigger picture when sampling habitats it is important to collect information on abiotic factors (physical) such as temperature, pH of soil and light intensity, as these will affect where the organisms live.

A quadrat

> The areas sampled may be unrepresentative of the whole area so it is important to take into account the limitations of these methods.

Pooters and pitfall traps

Counting plants is relatively easy, but animals tend to move around. Pooters can be used to collect animals

Keys 1

When animals and plants have been collected in a sample we can use keys to identify them.

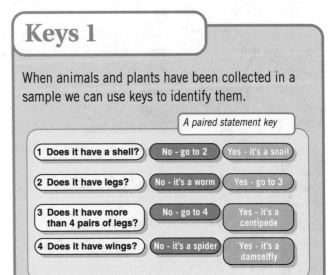

A paired statement key

1 Does it have a shell?	No - go to 2	Yes - it's a snail
2 Does it have legs?	No - it's a worm	Yes - go to 3
3 Does it have more than 4 pairs of legs?	No - go to 4	Yes - it's a centipede
4 Does it have wings?	No - it's a spider	Yes - it's a damselfly

Keys 2

A branching key

Has it got legs?

Yes → Has it got wings?

No → Has it got a shell?

Has it got wings?
Yes → **Damselfly**
No → Does it have more than four pairs of legs?

Has it got a shell?
Yes → **Snail**
No → **Worm**

Does it have more than four pairs of legs?
Yes → **Centipede**
No → **Spider**

Ecosystems

An ecosystem is made up of a moving, living part, known as the community, and a non-living part, called the habitat. The habitat is the place in which organisms live. It has all the conditions that they need to survive. A community is all the plants and animals that live in that habitat.

There are natural ecosystems, such as woodlands or lakes; or artificial ecosystems, such as greenhouses and aquariums. Artificial ecosystems tend to have less of a variety of organisms and may use weedkillers, pesticides and fertilisers.

Classification

Classification is a way of sorting living things into groups according to their similarities and differences. Carl Linnaeus devised a classification system based on features including body shape, types of limbs, and skeleton. The smallest group of living things is called a species and the largest are called kingdoms. This is the order of classification:

Kingdom
Phylum
Class
Order

Family
Genus
Species

Species

A species is a group of living things that are able to breed together to produce fertile offspring. Species contain animals or plants that have several features in common but show variation, as with different breeds of dog. Different species can be very similar and live in similar types of habitat. They may share a common ancestor.

An example of a species is the Galapagos finches studied by Charles Darwin. He analysed different varieties of finches and concluded that they shared a common ancestor. He noted, however, that they had evolved into different species as a result of living and adapting to different habitats by flying to various islands around the mainland.

Horses and donkeys are different species but they have many things in common. When they breed, however, their mule offspring are infertile.

Each species is given a **binomial**, a label that consists of two scientific names. The first name shows us what genus the species belongs to and the second records its species, e.g. *Homo sapiens* is the

binomial name for humans. The scientific name for an animal is used to avoid confusion, as the animal may be known by different names in different countries.

Kingdoms

For many years, only two major kingdoms were recognised: the animal kingdom and the plant kingdom. Today scientists recognise five kingdoms.

For many years fungi were classified as plants. They now belong in their own kingdom as they do not have chlorophyll and cannot make their own food by photosynthesis.

The animal kingdom is divided into vertebrates (animals with backbones) and invertebrates (animals without backbones).

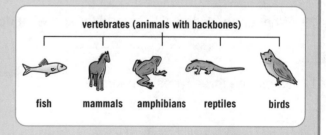

vertebrates (animals with backbones)

fish   mammals   amphibians   reptiles   birds

QUICK TEST

1. What methods are used to collect and study animals in a habitat?

2. What are abiotic factors?

3. What is the non-living part of an ecosystem called?

4. Who devised the classification system?

5. To which species does the animal *Canis familiaris* belong?

Practice questions

Use the questions to test your progress. Check your answers on page 125.

1. What is an indicator species?

....

2. Give an example of an intensive farming method.

....

3. Is a plant an autotroph or a heterotroph?

....

4. What was Dolly the sheep?

....

5. What was Mendel famous for?

....

6. How is the bacterial disease tuberculosis spread?

....

7. How can long-sightedness be corrected?

....

8. What is meant by the term 'active immunity'?

....

9. If you were to eat a diet rich in saturated fats what would the effects be?

....

10. What do the letters CNS stand for and what does it consist of?

....

11. Name the three types of neurone.

....

12. If a person had a grand mal seizure, what disorder of the brain would they suffer from?

....

13. Which hormone used to be extracted from a pig's pancreas?

....

14. What is the function of
    a) insulin
    b) glucagon?

....

....

15. Who discovered insulin?

    ....

16. Explain what a vector is and give an example.

    ....

17. Name the two types of white blood cell that protect us from disease.

    ....

18. Explain the term 'natural immunity'.

    ....

19. Define the word homeostasis.

    ....

20. Name a recessive inherited disease and a dominant inherited disease.

    ....

21. What are alternative forms of a gene called?

    ....

22. Which hormones are involved in the menstrual cycle?

    ....

23. What type of organisms do we use for genetic engineering?

    ....

24. What information does a pyramid of biomass tell us?

    ....

25. Who developed the theory of evolution that we use today?

    ....

26. Who developed an alternative theory of evolution?

    ....

27. List some ways in which energy is lost from a food chain.

    ....

28. Name three ways of sampling habitats.

    ....

29. What system did Carl Linnaeus develop?

    ....

30. Define the word species.

    ....

Limestone

Limestone is a *sedimentary* rock. It is mainly composed of the chemical calcium *carbonate*. It can be *quarried* and cut into blocks that can be used for *building*.

Rocks

Rocks can be classified into three groups: sedimentary, metamorphic and igneous. Marble is an example of a metamorphic rock. Marble is made when limestone is subjected to high pressures and temperatures.

Granite is an example of an igneous rock. Igneous rocks are the hardest type of rock, and metamorphic rocks are harder than sedimentary rocks.

> *If limestone is powdered it can be used to neutralise the acidity in lakes caused by acid rain and to neutralise acidic soils.*

Heating limestone

When **limestone** (calcium carbonate) is heated it breaks down to form **quicklime** (calcium oxide) and **carbon dioxide**.

calcium carbonate → calcium oxide + carbon dioxide
$$CaCO_{3(s)} \rightarrow CaO_{(s)} + CO_{2(g)}$$

This is an example of a **thermal decomposition** reaction.

Quicklime (calcium oxide) can be reacted with water to form **slaked lime (calcium hydroxide)**. A solution of slaked lime is known as limewater.

calcium oxide + water → calcium hydroxide
$$CaO_{(s)} + H_2O_{(l)} \rightarrow Ca(OH)_{2(s)}$$

The **thermal decomposition** of limestone is an example of a reaction that takes in heat. This is called an **endothermic** reaction.

> *The formula $CaCO_3$ shows us the type and ratio of atoms present. Here, the calcium, carbon and oxygen atoms are present in the ratio 1:1:3.*

Calcium oxide is an example of a compound that is held together by ionic bonds. Ionic bonding involves the **transfer of electrons**. This forms **ions** with opposite charges, which then **attract each other**.

> *Calcium oxide and calcium hydroxide are both bases and so can be used to neutralise acidic lakes and soils.*

Reaction summary

Limestone plus heat produces carbon dioxide.

Limestone is used to make slaked lime.

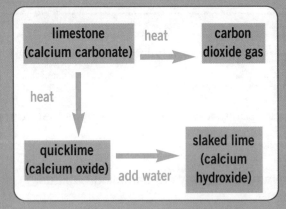

Similar thermal decomposition reactions 1

Other metal carbonates decompose in a **similar way** when they are heated. When copper carbonate is heated it breaks down to give copper oxide and carbon dioxide.

Similar thermal decomposition reactions 2

$$\text{copper carbonate} \rightarrow \text{copper oxide} + \text{carbon dioxide}$$
$$CuCO_3 \quad \rightarrow \quad CuO \quad + \quad CO_2$$

Heating baking powder

When **metal hydrogen carbonate compounds** are heated, they undergo thermal decomposition reactions to form **metal carbonates**, carbon dioxide and water.

The main chemical compound in baking powder is sodium hydrogen carbonate, $NaHCO_3$. When heated fiercely it reacts to form sodium carbonate, carbon dioxide and water.

$$\text{sodium hydrogen carbonate} \rightarrow \text{sodium carbonate} + \text{carbon dioxide} + \text{water}$$
$$2NaHCO_3 \quad \rightarrow \quad Na_2CO_3 + CO_2 + H_2O$$

Other uses of limestone

Limestone can be used to make other useful materials.

Cement

Cement is produced by **roasting powdered clay with powdered limestone** in a rotating kiln. If water is added and the mixture is allowed to set, it forms the hard, stone-like material, cement.

Mortar

When **water is mixed with cement and sand** and then allowed to set, mortar is made.

Concrete

Concrete is made by **mixing cement, sand and rock chippings with water**. When water is added to cement it hydrates and binds together all the particles to form a material that is as hard as rock. Concrete is tough and cheap and is widely used in building.

Glass

Glass can be made by **heating up a mixture of limestone (calcium carbonate), sand (silicon dioxide) and soda (sodium carbonate)** until the mixture melts.

Reinforced concrete is a useful composite material. It is made by allowing concrete to set around steel supports. This material combines the hardness of concrete with the flexibility of steel.

1. What is the main chemical in limestone?
2. What type of rock is limestone?
3. What type of rock is granite?
4. What is powdered limestone used for?
5. Give the word equation for the thermal decomposition of zinc carbonate.
6. What is the symbol equation for the thermal decomposition of zinc carbonate?
7. How is cement made?
8. How is glass made?
9. Name the three products formed by the thermal decomposition of sodium hydrogen carbonate.
10. What is the symbol equation for the thermal decomposition of sodium hydrogen carbonate?

Fuels

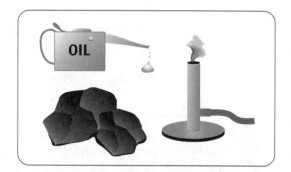

Fuels are burnt to release energy. In this country, the fossil fuels *coal*, *oil* and *natural gas* are widely used. The burning of fuels is an exothermic reaction.

Formation of coal, oil and natural gas

Fossil fuels are formed over **millions of years** from the fossilised remains of dead plants and animals. When plants and animals died, they fell to the sea or swamp floor. Their remains were quickly covered by sediment. In the absence of oxygen, the remains did not decay. Over time, more layers of sediment gradually built up and the lower layers became heated and pressurised. After millions of years, coal, oil and natural gas were formed. Fossil fuels are non-renewable, but are being used up very quickly.

💡 *Coal is mainly carbon. Petrol, diesel and oil are hydrocarbons.*

Fractional distillation of crude oil

Crude oil, like many natural substances is a **mixture**. The most important molecules in crude oil are called **hydrocarbons**. Hydrocarbons are molecules that only contain carbon and hydrogen atoms.

Some hydrocarbons have very short chains of carbon atoms. These hydrocarbons:

- are runny
- are easy to ignite
- have low boiling points
- are valuable fuels.

Other hydrocarbon molecules have much longer chains of carbon atoms. These hydrocarbon molecules:

- are more viscous (less runny)
- are harder to ignite
- have higher boiling points.

These longer hydrocarbon molecules are less useful as fuels. Before any of these hydrocarbon molecules can be used, however, they must first be separated into groups of molecules with a similar number of carbon atoms called **fractions**.

Crude oil can be separated by **fractional distillation**. First the crude oil is heated until it eventually evaporates. The diagram of the fractionating column shows that the bottom of the fractionating column is much hotter than the top of the column. This means that short hydrocarbon molecules can reach the top of the column before they condense and are collected. Longer hydrocarbon molecules condense at higher temperatures and are collected at different points down the column.

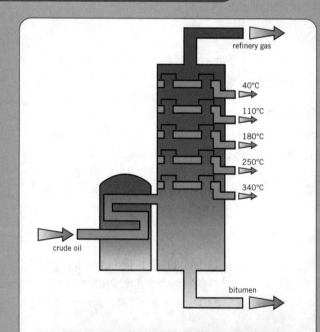

No. carbon atoms in hydrogen chain	Temperature	Fraction collected
3	less than 40°C	refinery gas
8	40°C	petrol
10	110°C	naphtha
15	180°C	kerosene
20	250°C	diesel
35	340°C	oil
50+	above 340°C	bitumen

How a fractionating column works

FUELS

Chemistry

Cracking

The large hydrocarbon molecules separated during the fractional distillation of crude oil are not very useful. These hydrocarbon molecules, however, can be broken down into smaller, more useful and so more valuable molecules by a process called **cracking**.

Cracking large hydrocarbon molecules can produce more useful products. Some of these molecules are used as fuels

Industrial cracking

- The cracking of long-chain hydrocarbons is carried out on a large scale.
- The long hydrocarbon molecules are heated until they evaporate.
- The vapour is then passed over a hot aluminium oxide catalyst.
- In this example, decane is being cracked to produce octane and ethene.

Octane is one of the hydrocarbon molecules in petrol. Ethene, a member of the alkene family of hydrocarbons, is also produced. Ethene is used to make a range of new compounds including plastics and industrial alcohol.

🛈 *Cracking is an example of a thermal decomposition reaction. Some of the products of the cracking are very useful fuels.*

decane $C_{10}H_{22}$ (from the naphtha fraction) $\rightarrow$ octane C_8H_{18} + ethene C_2H_4

$$H-\overset{\overset{H}{|}}{\underset{\underset{H}{|}}{C}}-\overset{\overset{H}{|}}{\underset{\underset{H}{|}}{C}}-\overset{\overset{H}{|}}{\underset{\underset{H}{|}}{C}}-\overset{\overset{H}{|}}{\underset{\underset{H}{|}}{C}}-\overset{\overset{H}{|}}{\underset{\underset{H}{|}}{C}}-\overset{\overset{H}{|}}{\underset{\underset{H}{|}}{C}}-\overset{\overset{H}{|}}{\underset{\underset{H}{|}}{C}}-\overset{\overset{H}{|}}{\underset{\underset{H}{|}}{C}}-\overset{\overset{H}{|}}{\underset{\underset{H}{|}}{C}}-\overset{\overset{H}{|}}{\underset{\underset{H}{|}}{C}}-H$$

$\rightarrow$

$$H-\overset{\overset{H}{|}}{\underset{\underset{H}{|}}{C}}-\overset{\overset{H}{|}}{\underset{\underset{H}{|}}{C}}-\overset{\overset{H}{|}}{\underset{\underset{H}{|}}{C}}-\overset{\overset{H}{|}}{\underset{\underset{H}{|}}{C}}-\overset{\overset{H}{|}}{\underset{\underset{H}{|}}{C}}-\overset{\overset{H}{|}}{\underset{\underset{H}{|}}{C}}-\overset{\overset{H}{|}}{\underset{\underset{H}{|}}{C}}-\overset{\overset{H}{|}}{\underset{\underset{H}{|}}{C}}-H$$

+

$$\underset{H}{\overset{H}{>}}C=C\underset{H}{\overset{H}{<}}$$

Cracking large hydrocarbon molecules can produce more useful products. Some of these molecules are used as fuels

QUICK TEST

1. Name three fossil fuels.

2. How long does it take for fossil fuels to form?

3. Which elements are found in hydrocarbon molecules?

4. Give three properties of short-chain hydrocarbon molecules.

5. Which hydrocarbons make the best fuels?

6. Where are the short-chain hydrocarbon molecules collected in a fractionating column?

7. Why are long-chain hydrocarbons cracked to form smaller ones?

8. What is the catalyst used in the industrial cracking of hydrocarbons?

9. What family does ethene belong to?

10. What does a 'fraction' mean in this context?

Organic families

Carbon atoms have the ability to form *four bonds* with other atoms. This means that carbon atoms can be made into a large range of compounds. These compounds are the basis of life and, because of this, the chemistry of these compounds is called *organic chemistry*.

Alkanes

The alkanes are a family of **hydrocarbon molecules**. This means that alkanes only contain hydrogen and carbon atoms. Scientists describe alkanes as **saturated** hydrocarbons. This is because they contain no C=C (double carbon) bonds and so already contain the maximum number of hydrogen atoms.

Alkanes are useful fuels. As they do not contain C=C bonds, they do not react with bromine water.

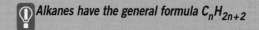 *Alkanes have the general formula C_nH_{2n+2}*

Name	methane	ethane	propane	butane
Chemical formula	CH_4	C_2H_6	C_3H_8	C_4H_{10}
Structure	H │ H–C–H │ H	H H │ │ H–C–C–H │ │ H H	H H H │ │ │ H–C–C–C–H │ │ │ H H H	H H H H │ │ │ │ H–C–C–C–C–H │ │ │ │ H H H H

Alkenes

The alkenes are also hydrocarbon molecules. Scientists describe alkenes as **unsaturated** hydrocarbons because they all contain one or more C=C (double carbon) bond.

Alkenes are more reactive than alkanes due to the presence of C=C bonds. This means alkenes are more useful because they can be used to make new substances. Alkenes do react with **bromine water**. Bromine water decolourises in the presence of alkenes.

Alkenes have the general formula C_nH_{2n}

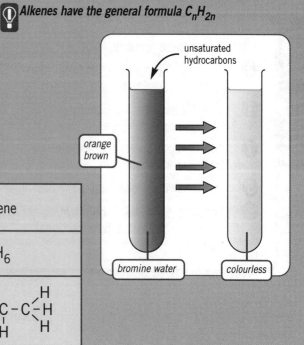

Name	ethene	propene
Chemical formula	C_2H_4	C_3H_6

Structure	H H
	  \\ /
	   C=C
	  / \\
	H H
		H H
		  \\ /
		   C=C–C–H
		  / │ \\
		H H H

Alcohols

The term alcohol is often used for the compound **ethanol**. In fact, ethanol is just one member of a family of organic compounds called alcohols. All alcohols have an **–OH group**. Each member of the family differs from the previous one by the addition of a CH_2 group.

Covalent bonding

These compounds all contain covalent bonds.

Covalent bonding involves the sharing of electrons. The shared pairs of electrons hold the atoms together.

Name	methanol	ethanol
Chemical formula	CH_3OH	C_2H_5OH
Structure	H | H–C–O–H | H	H H | | H–C–C–O–H | | H H

Carboxylic acids

Carboxylic acids are a family of organic compounds with the functional group **–COOH**. Carboxylic acids are weak acids that react with metals, alkalis and carbonates. They have rather unpleasant smells. The well-known carboxylic acid, **ethanoic acid**, is found in vinegar.

The carboxylic acid, ethanoic acid, is found in vinegar

Name	methanoic acid	ethanoic acid
Chemical formula	HCOOH	CH_3COOH
Structure	H–C (=O) OH	H–C–C (=O) O–H

Esters

Esters are a family of organic compounds formed when alcohols react with carboxylic acids. Esters have **pleasant fruity smells and flavours** and are used widely in cheap perfumes and to flavour foods.

ethanol + ethanoic acid → ethyl ethanoate + water

The ester, ethyl ethanoate, is formed when ethanol is reacted with ethanoic acid using an acid catalyst.

QUICK TEST

1. How many bonds do carbon atoms form?
2. Why are alkanes described as saturated hydrocarbons?
3. What is the name of the first member of the alkane family?
4. Draw the structure of the first four members of the alkane family.
5. Draw the structure of the first two members of the alkene family.
6. Which family does ethene belong to?
7. How could you differentiate between an alkane and an alkene?
8. What is the general formula for an alkane?
9. Which hydrocarbon family does the compound ethanol belong to?
10. What is the formula of ethanol?

Vegetable oils

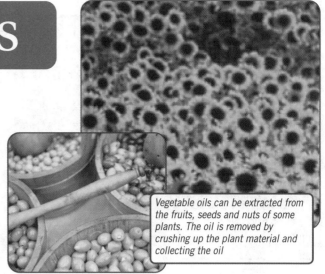

Plant oils are a valuable source of *energy* in our diets. They are also essential sources of vitamins A and D.

Vegetable oils can be produced from the *fruits*, *seeds or nuts* of some plants. Popular vegetable oils include olive oil and sunflower oil.

Vegetable oils can be extracted from the fruits, seeds and nuts of some plants. The oil is removed by crushing up the plant material and collecting the oil

Using fats for cooking

Fats have **higher boiling points** than water. Cooking food by frying is therefore much faster than cooking food by boiling. In addition, frying foods produces interesting **new flavours** and **increases the energy content** of the food.

Frying potatoes to make chips

Fuels

When vegetable oils are burnt, they release lots of energy. In fact, vegetable oils can be used in place of fossil fuels in the production of **bio-diesel**. This is an alternative to normal diesel that is produced from the fossil fuel crude oil.

What is a fat molecule?

Fats and oils are complex molecules.

Saturated and unsaturated fats

Animal fats are usually **solid**, or nearly solid, at room temperature. A saturated fat contains many C–C bonds but **no C=C** bonds. Scientists believe that people who eat lots of saturated fats may develop raised blood cholesterol levels. This is linked with an increased risk of heart disease.

Most vegetable fats are liquids at room temperature and so are described as oils.

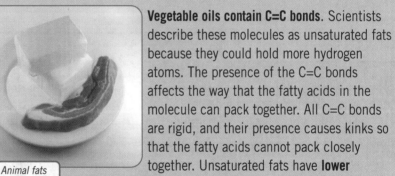

Animal fats

Vegetable oils contain C=C bonds. Scientists describe these molecules as unsaturated fats because they could hold more hydrogen atoms. The presence of the C=C bonds affects the way that the fatty acids in the molecule can pack together. All C=C bonds are rigid, and their presence causes kinks so that the fatty acids cannot pack closely together. Unsaturated fats have **lower melting points** than saturated fats. While most vegetable fats are **liquid at room temperature**, most animal fats are solids.

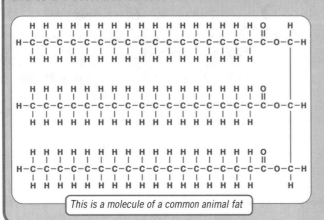

This is a molecule of a common animal fat

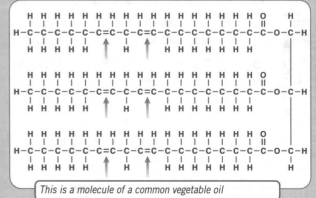

This is a molecule of a common vegetable oil

Polyunsaturated fats

Some unsaturated fats have just one C=C bond in the fatty acid chain. These are described as monounsaturated fats.

Other unsaturated fats have **many C=C** bonds. These are known as **polyunsaturated fats**. Scientists believe that polyunsaturated fats are better for people's health.

Emulsion

Salad dressing is an example of a type of everyday mixture called an emulsion. It is a **mixture of two liquids**: oil and vinegar. Salad dressing is made by shaking oil and vinegar so that they mix together. After a short while, however, the oil and vinegar **separate out to form two distinct layers**. Many of the salad dressings bought from shops contain molecules called emulsifiers that help the oil and vinegar to stay mixed together. Emulsifiers are molecules with two very different ends. One end is attracted to oil, while the other end is attracted to the water in the vinegar. The addition of emulsifiers keeps the two liquids mixed together.

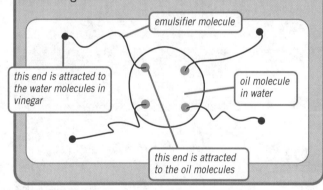

emulsifier molecule

this end is attracted to the water molecules in vinegar

oil molecule in water

this end is attracted to the oil molecules

Food additives

Scientists often add chemicals to improve foods. The chemicals that have passed safety tests and are approved for use throughout the European Union are called 'E-numbers'. Chemicals that are commonly added to foods include:

- emulsifiers, which help ingredients to mix together
- colours, which are added to make food look more attractive
- flavours, which are added to enhance taste
- artificial sweeteners, which are used to decrease the amount of sugar used.

Hydrogenated vegetable oils

Vegetable oils are often liquids at room temperature because they contain C=C bonds. There are, however, advantages to using fats that are solid at room temperature. They are easier to spread and can be used to make new products like cakes and pastries.

Vegetable oils can be made solid at room temperature by a process known as **hydrogenation**. The oils are heated with **hydrogen and a nickel catalyst**. The hydrogen atoms add across double bonds to form fats that are solid at room temperature. In addition, hydrogenated vegetable oils have a longer shelf life.

Margarine is one example of a hydrogenated vegetable oil

QUICK TEST

1. Which parts of plants can we obtain oils from?
2. Which part of a sunflower is used to obtain oil?
3. Which vitamins do we obtain from eating fats?
4. Why is frying food faster than boiling food?
5. Will a food that has been fried or a food that has been boiled contain more energy?
6. If a fat is a solid at room temperature, would you expect it to be saturated or unsaturated?
7. What do polyunsaturated fats have?
8. What are the advantages of having fats that are solid at room temperature?
9. What is the catalyst used in the hydrogenation of vegetable oil to produce margarine?
10. Why are artificial sweeteners added to foods?

Plastics

Many molecules can be joined together to make one big molecule.

Polymerisation

$$n \quad \underset{H}{\overset{H}{C}} = \underset{H}{\overset{H}{C}} \rightarrow \left(\underset{H}{\overset{H}{C}} - \underset{H}{\overset{H}{C}} \right)_n$$

Notice the 'n' at the start of the equation and the section of the polymer surrounded by brackets. The 'n' represents the number of molecules involved

We have seen how the simplest alkene, **ethene**, can be formed by the cracking of large hydrocarbon molecules. If ethene is heated under pressure in the presence of a catalyst, many ethene molecules can join together to form a larger molecule called poly(ethene) or **polythene**.

Here we can see how a large number of ethene molecules join together to form polythene.

The brackets are used because it would be impractical to write out the complete structure. The brackets surround a representative unit that is repeated through the whole polymer.

The small starting molecules, in this case the ethene molecules, are called **monomers**. The C=C bonds in the ethene molecules join together to form long chain molecules called **polymers**. A polymer, therefore, is made from lots of monomer units. In fact, 'poly' means 'many'. This is an example of an addition polymerisation reaction.

The ethene molecules have simply joined together.

Other polymers

Polymerisation reactions may involve other monomer units. The exact properties of the polymer formed depend upon:

- the monomers involved
- the conditions under which it was made.

Polypropene

Polypropene is made by an addition polymerisation reaction between **many propene** molecules.

$$n \quad \underset{H}{\overset{CH_3}{C}} = \underset{H}{\overset{H}{C}} \rightarrow \left(\underset{H}{\overset{CH_3}{C}} - \underset{H}{\overset{H}{C}} \right)_n$$

Many propene molecules join together to form polypropene

$$n \quad \underset{H}{\overset{Cl}{C}} = \underset{H}{\overset{H}{C}} \rightarrow \left(\underset{H}{\overset{Cl}{C}} - \underset{H}{\overset{H}{C}} \right)_n$$

Many chloroethene (vinyl chloride) molecules join together to form polyvinyl chloride

Polyvinyl chloride (PVC)

Polyvinyl chloride is made by an addition polymerisation reaction between **many chloroethene** molecules.

Chloroethene used to be called vinyl chloride.

Polytetrafluoroethene (PTFE or Teflon)

Polytetrafluoroethene is made by an addition polymerisation reaction between **many tetrafluoroethene** molecules.

$$n \quad \underset{F}{\overset{F}{C}} = \underset{F}{\overset{F}{C}} \rightarrow \left(\underset{F}{\overset{F}{C}} - \underset{F}{\overset{F}{C}} \right)_n$$

Many tetrafluoroethene molecules join together to form polytetrafluoroethene (PTFE)

Thermoplastics and thermosetting plastics 1

Thermoplastics consist of long polymer chains with **few cross-links**.

When heated, these chains untangle and the material softens. **It can then be reshaped.** On cooling, the material becomes solid and stiff again. Thermoplastics can be heated and reshaped many times. Polythene is a thermoplastic.

Thermosetting plastics consist of long, **heavily cross-linked** polymer chains.

When they are first made, these plastics are soft and can be shaped. Once they have set, however, they become solid and soft. **They do not soften again** even if they are heated to very high temperatures and so they cannot be reshaped. Melamine is a thermosetting plastic.

Thermoplastics and thermosetting plastics 2

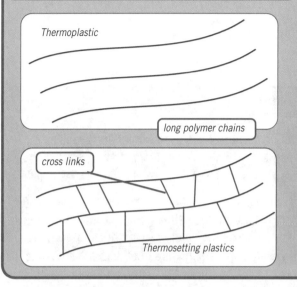

Thermoplastic

long polymer chains

cross links

Thermosetting plastics

New polymers

Scientists are **developing new and exciting polymers**.

Hydrogels are an example of these new types of polymers. Hydrogels are able to bind water and are being used to make special wound dressings to help injured people. Hydrogels help to:

■ stop fluid loss from the wound
■ absorb bacteria and odour molecules
■ cool and cushion the wound
■ reduce the number of times the wound has to be disturbed - the hydrogel is transparent and so doctors and nurses can monitor the wound without having to remove the dressing.

Uses of plastics

Polythene

Polythene is cheap and strong.

It is used to make plastic bags and bottles.

PVC

PVC is rigid and can be used to make building materials such as drainpipes.

Chemicals called plasticisers can be added to PVC to make products like Wellington boots and mackintoshes.

Polypropene

Polypropene is strong and has a high elasticity.

It is used to make crates and ropes.

Polystyrene

Polystyrene is cheap and can be moulded into different shapes.

It is used for packaging and for plastic casings.

🛈 *Know the properties and uses of different plastics.*

Scientific processes

The problems caused by plastics that do not breakdown in the environment have encouraged scientists to design new biodegradable plastics.

QUICK TEST

1. Draw a diagram to show how polythene is formed from ethene.

2. Draw a diagram to show how polypropene is formed from propene.

3. What type of reaction is involved in the formation of polythene?

4. What is the name given to the small units that join together to form a polymer?

5. Which family of plastics can only be shaped once?

6. What type of plastic is melamine?

7. Which plastic is cheap and strong?

8. Which plastic has high elasticity?

9. Which plastic is used to make milk crates?

Ethanol

Ethanol is a member of the alcohol family of organic compounds.

Uses of ethanol

Ethanol has the following structure.

```
    H   H
    |   |
H — C — C — O — H
    |   |
    H   H
```

The structure of ethanol

Ethanol is found in drinks like beer and wine. It is, however, toxic in large amounts. Ethanol has many useful properties. It is a **good solvent** and evaporates quickly. Many aftershaves contain ethanol. Ethanol is an important raw material and can also be used as a **fuel**.

Methanol is another member of the alcohol group and is even more toxic than ethanol. If someone was to drink methanol, they could become blind or even die. Methylated spirit is a mixture of ethanol, methanol and a purple dye. The purple dye is there to warn people about its toxicity; and its unpleasant taste is there to try and stop people from drinking it.

Ethanol as a fuel

In some countries, alcohol made from sugar beet or sugar cane is made into alcohol. This alcohol can then be mixed with petrol to produce a fuel for vehicles like cars. Ethanol is a **renewable energy** resource that burns very cleanly. **Alcohols**, however, **release less energy** than petrol when they are burnt. In order to produce enough alcohol for fuel, large areas of fertile land would be required to grow the plants needed to produce the alcohol.

Sugar cane can be used to produce alcohol which can be burnt as a fuel

Fermentation

Fermentation has been used to make alcohol for thousands of years. We use fermentation to make alcoholic drinks. Fruits, vegetables and cereals are all sources of the sugar glucose, $C_6H_{12}O_6$.

During fermentation, **yeast** is used to catalyse (speed up) the reaction in which glucose is converted into ethanol and carbon dioxide.

$$\text{yeast}$$
$$\text{glucose} \rightarrow \text{ethanol} + \text{carbon dioxide}$$
$$C_6H_{12}O_6 \rightarrow 2C_2H_5OH + 2CO_2$$

The temperature of the reaction has to be carefully controlled. If the temperature falls too low, the yeast becomes inactive and the rate of the reaction slows down. If the temperature is too high, the yeast enzymes are denatured and stop working altogether, or the yeast may be killed.

Ethanol, produced by fermentation, has a concentration of around 6 to 14%. Some people prefer drinks with higher alcohol content. These higher concentrations of alcohol are achieved by a process called **fractional distillation**. There is a very strong link, however, between the consumption of alcohol and an increased risk of accidents and raised levels of crime. Some religions prohibit the consumption of all alcoholic drinks altogether.

> *Yeast is an enzyme or biological catalyst. It speeds up the conversion of sugar to alcohol and carbon dioxide, but is not itself used up in the process.*

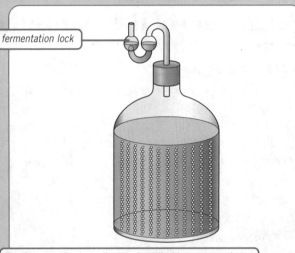

fermentation lock

The fermentation lock allows carbon dioxide to escape, but stops oxygen in the air from reaching the alcohol. This is important as ethanol can easily be oxidised to form ethanoic acid, which would make the drink taste sour

Industrial alcohol

There is another, more modern way of producing vast amounts of alcohol. During this method, **ethene** (which is produced during the cracking of long-chain hydrocarbons) is **reacted with steam to produce ethanol**.

$$\text{ethene} + \text{steam} \rightarrow \text{ethanol}$$
$$C_2H_4 + H_2O \rightarrow C_2H_5OH$$

A catalyst of **phosphoric acid and a temperature of 300°C** are used.

This method of producing ethanol is much cheaper than fermentation. Our reserves of fossil fuels are, however, finite and will run out one day.

Evolution of the atmosphere

Today the atmosphere is composed of:

- about 80% nitrogen

- about 20% oxygen

- small amounts of other gases such as carbon dioxide, water vapour and noble gases (e.g. argon).

This has not always been the case. Throughout the history of the Earth the composition of the atmosphere has changed and evolved.

Formation of the atmosphere

The first billion years

- During the first billion years of the Earth's life, there was **enormous volcanic activity**.

- Volcanoes belched out carbon dioxide (CO_2), steam (H_2O), ammonia (NH_3) and methane (CH_4).

- The atmosphere consisted **mainly of carbon dioxide** and there was very little oxygen. In fact, Earth's atmosphere was very similar to the atmosphere of the planets **Mars and Venus** today.

- The steam condensed to form the early oceans.

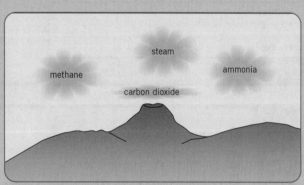

Later

- During the two billion years that followed, **plants evolved** and began to cover the surface of the Earth.

- The plants grew very well in the carbon dioxide rich atmosphere. They steadily removed carbon dioxide and produced oxygen (O_2).

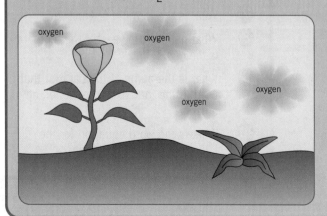

Later still

- Most of the carbon from the carbon dioxide in the early atmosphere gradually became **locked up** as carbonate minerals and fossil fuels in sedimentary rocks.

- The ammonia in the early atmosphere reacted with oxygen to release nitrogen.

- Living organisms, such as denitrifying bacteria, also produced nitrogen.

- As the amount of oxygen increased, an **ozone layer** (O_3) developed. This layer filtered out harmful ultraviolet radiation from the Sun, enabling new, more complex life forms to develop.

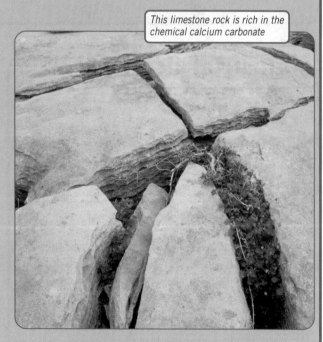

This limestone rock is rich in the chemical calcium carbonate

Is burning fossil fuels going to cause problems?

The level of carbon dioxide in our atmosphere has increased since the Industrial Revolution as we have burnt more fossil fuels. These fossil fuels had stored carbon dioxide from the Earth's early atmosphere for hundreds of millions of years.

There is a mismatch, however, between the amount of carbon dioxide released into the atmosphere by the burning of fossil fuels and the actual increase in the amount of carbon dioxide in the atmosphere. A great deal of the carbon dioxide appears to be missing. Scientists believe that much of the carbon dioxide produced is removed from the atmosphere by the **reaction between carbon dioxide and seawater**. This reaction produces:

- **insoluble carbonate** salts which are deposited as sediment
- **soluble calcium and magnesium hydrogen carbonate** salts which sometimes end up as sediment.

Much of the carbon dioxide is, therefore, locked up in sediment for long periods of time. Some of this carbon dioxide is later released back into the atmosphere when the sediment is sub-ducted underground by geological activity and then becomes involved in volcanoes.

However, not all of the carbon dioxide released by the burning of fossil fuels is removed in these ways. Many people are concerned about rising levels of carbon dioxide in the Earth's atmosphere and the possible link between these increased levels and global warming.

Scientific processes

Our theories about the evolution of the Earth's atmosphere come from scientific studies of rocks formed millions of years ago. Our ideas evolve as more evidence becomes available.

1. Approximately how much of today's atmosphere is made up of oxygen?

2. What is the main gas in the atmosphere today?

3. What other gases are present in small amounts in the Earth's atmosphere?

4. Which gases formed the Earth's early atmosphere?

5. Which was the main gas in the Earth's early atmosphere?

6. How did the evolution of plants affect the Earth's atmosphere?

7. What happened to most of the carbon dioxide in the Earth's early atmosphere?

8. What does the ozone layer do?

9. How did the development of the ozone layer affect life on Earth?

10. Why is the amount of carbon dioxide in the Earth's atmosphere increasing?

Pollution of the atmosphere

The atmosphere can be polluted in many ways.

Acid rain

Fossil fuels like coal, oil and natural gas often contain small amounts of **sulphur**. When these fuels are burnt, the gas **sulphur dioxide**, SO_2, is produced. This gas can dissolve in rainwater to form sulphuric acid and so **acid rain**. Acid rain can affect the environment by damaging statues and buildings, as well as harming plant and aquatic life.

Reducing acid rain

The amount of acid rain produced can be reduced in several ways. The easiest way is simply to **use less electricity** by turning off lights when they are not in use and not leaving everyday appliances on standby mode.

Alternatively, sulphur compounds can be **removed directly from oil and natural gas** before they are burnt so that they do not produce sulphur dioxide as they burn. The sulphur that is removed is a valuable material that can also be sold.

It is more difficult to remove sulphur from the fossil fuel coal. Alternatively, the sulphur dioxide produced by coal can be **removed from the waste gases** before they are released into the atmosphere. This process is carried out by scrubbers in power stations. The scrubbers react sulphur dioxide (from the waste gases) with calcium carbonate to produce gypsum and carbon dioxide.

Carbon monoxide

The gas carbon monoxide, or CO, can also cause problems. When fossil fuels containing carbon and hydrogen are burnt, the gases carbon dioxide and water vapour are produced. However, if carbon is burnt in an **insufficient supply of oxygen**, the gas carbon monoxide can also be produced.

Carbon monoxide is colourless, odourless and very poisonous. Faulty gas appliances can produce carbon monoxide and so it is important that they are regularly serviced.

Incomplete combustion is undesirable because:
- *it produces carbon monoxide*
- *less heat than expected is given off when the fuel is burnt*
- *soot is produced which must then be cleaned. A sooty flame has a yellow colour.*

Global dimming

Global dimming is caused by **smoke particles** that are released into the atmosphere. Scientists believe that these smoke particles reduce the amount of sunlight that reaches the Earth's surface and may even affect weather patterns.

Carbon dioxide and the greenhouse effect

The greenhouse effect is slowly heating up the Earth.

- When fossil fuels are burnt, the gas carbon dioxide is produced.
- Although some of this carbon dioxide is removed from the atmosphere by the reaction between carbon dioxide and seawater, the overall amount of carbon dioxide in the atmosphere has increased over the last 200 years.
- Carbon dioxide **traps the heat energy** that has reached the Earth from the Sun.
- Global warming may mean that the polar icecaps will eventually melt and this could cause massive flooding.

💡 *Plants use the gas carbon dioxide during photosynthesis.*

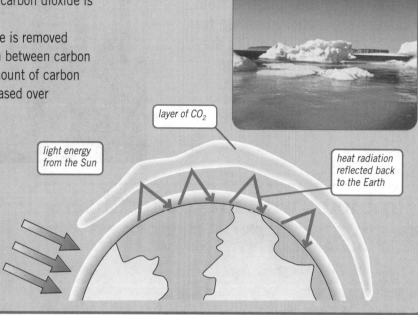

light energy from the Sun

layer of CO_2

heat radiation reflected back to the Earth

Catalytic converters

In this country all new, petrol-fuelled cars are fitted with catalytic converters or 'cats'. The 'cat' is part of a car's exhaust system and helps to **reduce the amount of harmful gases** that the car releases into the atmosphere. Catalytic converters work in several ways:

- they help to convert carbon monoxide to carbon dioxide
- they help to convert nitrogen oxides to nitrogen and oxygen
- they oxidise unburnt hydrocarbons to carbon dioxide and water vapour.

💡 *Nitrogen oxide is produced when fuels are burnt in air. The nitrogen oxide reacts with oxygen to form nitrogen dioxide. Nitrogen oxide and nitrogen dioxide are referred to as nitrogen oxides or 'NOx'.*

Catalytic converter

Scientific processes

Not all scientists believe that human activity is causing global warming. Other factors, such as solar cycles, may also be important. Until we have more evidence we will not really know.

QUICK TEST

1. What is the name of the gas produced when sulphur is burnt?
2. Which fossil fuel contains the most sulphur?
3. How can switching off lights prevent the formation of acid rain?
4. How can you tell that a fuel is being burnt in a poor supply of oxygen?
5. What gas is produced when carbon is burnt in a good supply of oxygen?
6. What gas is produced when carbon is burnt in an insufficient supply of oxygen?
7. What causes global dimming?
8. What are the problems associated with global dimming?
9. Which gas is linked to the greenhouse effect?
10. What device is fitted to a car's exhaust system to reduce the levels of harmful pollutants that a car releases into the atmosphere?

Pollution of the environment

All substances are obtained from, or made from matter obtained from the Earth's crust, the sea, or the atmosphere. It is vital that we protect the environment from harmful pollution.

Problems with nitrate fertilisers

Nitrate fertilisers can cause problems if they are washed into lakes or streams.

- Algae (small plants) thrive in the fertiliser-rich water and grow very well.
- Eventually, the algae die and bacteria start to decompose (break down) the algae.
- As the bacteria decompose, the algae use up all the oxygen in the water.
- Fish and other aquatic life cannot get enough oxygen and so they die.

This process is called **eutrophication**.

Nitrate fertilisers can also find their way into our drinking water supplies. There have been health concerns over the levels of nitrate in water and the prevalence of stomach cancer and 'blue baby' disease. Although no firm links have yet been proved, it seems wise that the **levels of nitrate in drinking water should be limited** until more is known.

Eutrophication

Problems with bauxite quarrying

Aluminium is used to make drinks cans

Aluminium is extracted from its ore, **bauxite**. Unfortunately, this ore is often found in environmentally sensitive areas like the Amazonian **rainforest**. Bauxite is extracted from large opencast mines. Large numbers of trees must be cut down to clear space for the mine and the new roads built to give access to the mine. In addition, litter and oil can pollute the area around the mine.

Aluminium can be recycled, however. This cuts down on landfill in this country and helps to preserve the Amazonian rainforests.

Problems with limestone quarrying

Limestone is a very important raw material. The economic benefits of quarrying for limestone, however, must be balanced against the social and environmental consequences of quarrying. Limestone has to be blasted from hillsides in huge quantities. This **scars the landscape, causes noise pollution and dust, and affects local wildlife**. Transporting limestone from the quarry can also cause problems, with **heavy lorries causing** **noise, congestion and damaging local roads**. Quarrying does, however, create new **jobs** and brings new **money** into an area.

Problems disposing of plastic

Plastics are very useful materials.

- They are very stable and unreactive.
- Most plastics do not react with water, oxygen or other common chemicals.
- Plastics are also **non-biodegradable**, which means that they are not decomposed by micro-organisms.

As a result, when plastic objects are no longer needed, they do not rot away. They remain in the environment and may cause problems. Plastic objects now fill many landfill sites.

We can get rid of plastics by burning them, but this solution may also cause problems. Although some plastics burn quite easily, they can give off harmful gases. The common plastic, PVC, releases the gas hydrogen chloride when it is burnt.

In response to these problems, scientists have developed new, biodegradable plastics that will eventually rot away.

This plastic bag is 100% degradable* but you can still reuse it!

*From date of manufacture, the plastic will start to degrade in approx. 18 months time. The whole process will take about 3 years. See bottom of bag for date of manufacture.

epi

QUICK TEST

1. In what products are nitrate chemicals found?
2. What happens when algae die?
3. Which two health problems have been linked to high levels of nitrates in drinking water?
4. Name the main ore of aluminium.
5. Name one place where aluminium ore can be mined.
6. How can we help reduce landfill and preserve rainforests?
7. How can limestone extraction affect the landscape?
8. What are the advantages of a new, local limestone quarry?
9. What is the name used to describe materials that are not broken down by micro-organisms?
10. What harmful gas is produced when PVC is burnt?

Evidence for plate tectonics

Silicon, oxygen and aluminium are all abundant in the Earth's crust.

Structure of the Earth

- Scientists believe that the Earth has a layered structure.
- The outer layer of **crust** is very thin and has a low density.
- The next layer down is called the **mantle**. This layer extends almost halfway to the centre of the Earth. The rock in the mantle is mainly solid, but small amounts must be liquid as the mantle flows very slowly.
- At the centre of the Earth is the **core**. The core consists of two parts. The outer core is liquid and the inner core, which is under even greater pressure, is solid.

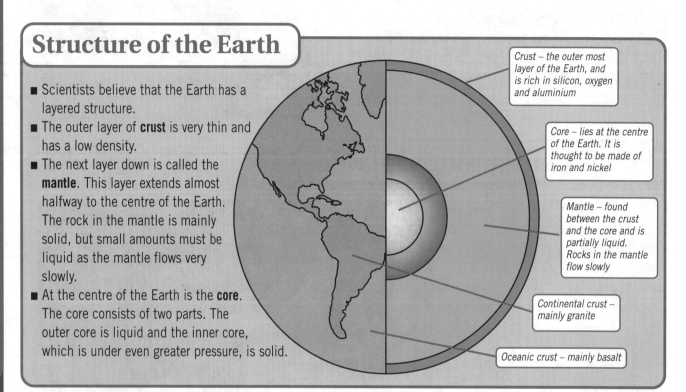

Crust – the outer most layer of the Earth, and is rich in silicon, oxygen and aluminium

Core – lies at the centre of the Earth. It is thought to be made of iron and nickel

Mantle – found between the crust and the core and is partially liquid. Rocks in the mantle flow slowly

Continental crust – mainly granite

Oceanic crust – mainly basalt

Evidence of the structure of the Earth

Evidence for the layered structure of the Earth comes from studies of the way that seismic waves (the shock waves sent out by earthquakes) travel through the Earth. The material through which they are travelling affects the speed of these waves. These studies show that the outer core of the Earth is liquid while the inner core is solid. The overall density of the Earth is greater than the density of the rocks that make up the Earth's crust. This means that the rocks in the mantle and the core must be much denser than the rocks we observe in the crust. Scientists believe that the core is mainly made of **iron and nickel**.

Movement of the crust 1

People used to believe that the features of the Earth's surface, such as the mountain ranges, were formed when the surface of the Earth shrank as it cooled down. However, scientists now believe that the Earth's geological features can be explained by using a single, unifying theory called **plate tectonics**.

The scientist Alfred Wegener first proposed the ideas behind plate tectonics. Initially these ideas were resisted, particularly by religious groups, but as more evidence emerged, the theory of plate tectonics was gradually accepted.

The main idea behind plate tectonics is that the Earth's **lithosphere** (crust and upper mantle) is split up into 12 large plates. Each of these plates moves slowly over the Earth's surface at a rate of a few centimetres a year.

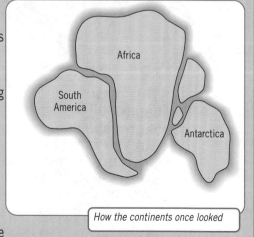

How the continents once looked

Movement of the crust 2

The movement of the plates is caused by **convection currents in the mantle**. These currents are caused by the **natural radioactive decay** of elements deep inside the Earth which release heat energy.

At one time, all the continents were joined together to form a super continent called Pangea. Since that time, the continents have moved apart and are now at their maximum separation.

Evidence that supports the theory of plate tectonics

There are many clues that support our ideas about plate tectonics:

1 When the South American coast was first mapped, people noticed that the east coast of South America and the west coast of Africa fitted together like pieces of an enormous **jigsaw**.

2 The examination of **fossil remains** in South America and Africa showed that rocks of the same age contained the remains of an unusual freshwater crocodile-type creature.

3 Further evidence that South America and Africa were once joined was uncovered when scientists discovered that **rock strata** of the same age were strikingly similar on both sides of the Atlantic.

4 British rocks that were created in the Carboniferous period (300 million years ago) must have formed in tropical swamps. Yet rocks found in Britain, which formed 200 million years ago, must have formed in deserts. This shows that Britain must have moved through **different climatic zones** as the tectonic plate that Britain rests on moved across the Earth's surface.

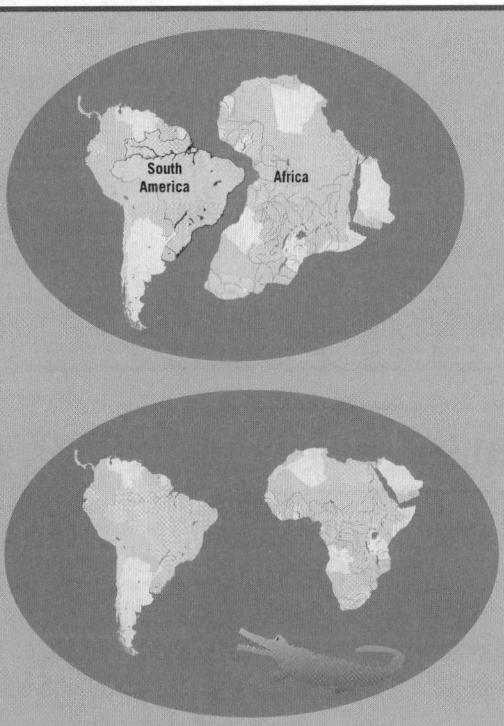

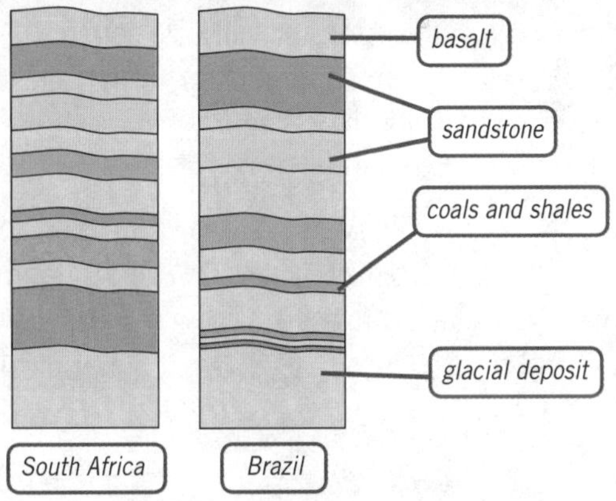

basalt

sandstone

coals and shales

glacial deposit

South Africa   Brazil

Rock strata from either side of the Atlantic

Scientific process

Our ideas about plate tectonics have changed over time. Scientists build a model that fits with the evidence currently available to them. When new evidence is discovered they must re-evaluate their existing models and, if necessary, change them to take in the new evidence.

QUICK TEST

1 What name is given to the outer layer of the Earth?

2 In which state is the Earth's inner core?

3 Which elements are abundant in the Earth's crust?

4 Which elements are abundant in the Earth's core?

5 How fast do tectonic plates move?

6 What is the Earth's lithosphere?

7 Historically, how did people once believe that mountain ranges formed?

8 What produces the heat that drives the plates' movements?

9 What is strange about the coastlines of South America and Africa?

10 How did fossil records provide evidence of plate tectonics?

Consequences of plate tectonics

The movement of tectonic plates causes many problems, including earthquakes and volcanoes. These tend to be worse near the edges of plates, known as the *plate boundaries*.

Plate movements

The plates can move in three different ways.

- They can slide past each other.
- They can move towards each other.
- They can move away from each other.

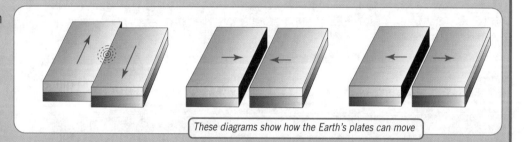

These diagrams show how the Earth's plates can move

Earthquakes

Earthquakes are caused by tectonic plates sliding past each other. The San Andreas Fault in California is a famous example of where this is occurring. The plates in this area have fractured into a very complicated pattern. As the plates try to move past each other, they tend to stick together rather than slide smoothly past. When the **plates stick together, forces build up**, until eventually the **plates move suddenly**. The strain that has built up is released in the form of an earthquake. If this happens beneath the oceans, it can result in catastrophic tsunami waves.

Scientists have studied earthquakes in an effort to predict exactly when they might occur and so warn people to move away from the affected areas. However, with so many factors involved, it is not always possible to predict exactly when an earthquake will occur. When they do happen, they can cause massive destruction and loss of life.

Earthquakes can cause enormous damage. This photograph was taken in Los Angeles after the 1994 earthquake

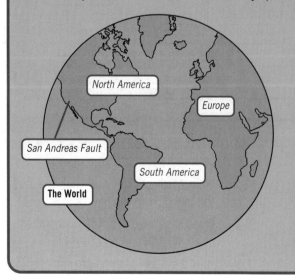

North America

Europe

San Andreas Fault

South America

The World

Volcanoes 1

Volcanoes are found in locations around the Earth where two plates are moving towards each other.

- These convergent plate boundaries often involve the collision between an **oceanic and a continental plate**.
- Oceanic plates contain minerals that are rich in the elements iron and magnesium, and are **denser** than continental plates.

Volcanoes 2

- When an oceanic plate and a continental plate converge, the denser, oceanic plate is forced beneath the continental plate.
- The continental plate is stressed, and the existing rocks are folded and metamorphosed.
- As the oceanic plate is forced down beneath the continental plate, sea water lowers the melting point of the rock and some of the oceanic plate may melt to form magma. This magma can rise up through cracks to form volcanoes.
- As the plates are moving past each other, earthquakes are also common in these areas.
- A convergent plate boundary along the western coast of South America is responsible for the formation of the Andes mountain range.

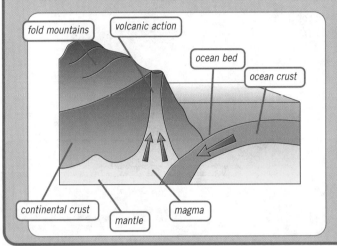

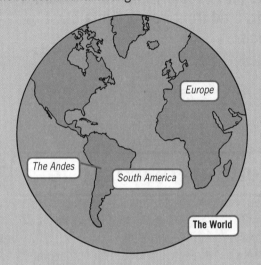

Mid-ocean ridge basalts

Another consequence of plate tectonics is the formation of mid-ocean ridge basalts.

When tectonic plates move apart, magma comes to the surface. This usually occurs under oceans. As the molten rock cools, it solidifies and forms the igneous rock, **basalt**. These plate boundaries are often referred to as constructive plate boundaries, because new crust is being made. Basalt is rich in iron, which is magnetic. As the basalt cools down, **the iron rich minerals in the basalt line up with the Earth's magnetic field**. By examining the direction in which these minerals have lined up, scientists are able to work out the direction of the Earth's magnetic field. However, examination of the basalt rocks on either side of a mid-ocean ridge shows **a striped magnetic reversal pattern**. The pattern is symmetrical about the ridge and

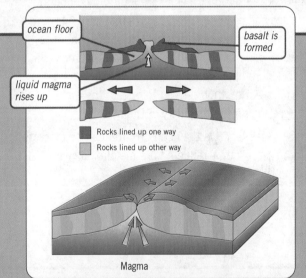

provides evidence that the Earth's magnetic field periodically changes direction. This reversal appears to be very sudden and to occur about every half a million years. According to the rock record, another reversal is now well overdue!

QUICK TEST

1. What are the three ways in which plates can move?
2. What causes earthquakes?
3. Why can't scientists predict the exact date of an earthquake?
4. Where is the San Andreas Fault?
5. How is magma formed when two plates converge?
6. Why do earthquakes sometimes occur near volcanoes?
7. Which element is abundant in basalt?
8. What affects the iron-rich minerals in basalt?

Extraction of iron

Iron is an *element*. Elements are substances that are made up of only one type of atom. There are only about 100 different elements.

Iron is an extremely important metal. It is extracted from iron ore in a blast furnace.

Methods of extraction

- The more reactive a metal is, the harder it is to remove it from its compound.
- Gold is so unreactive that it is found uncombined.
- However, all other metals are found in compounds. Occasionally we may find rocks that contain metals in such high concentrations that it is economically worthwhile to extract the metal from the rock. Such rocks are called **ores**.
- The exact method chosen to extract the metal depends on the reactivity of the metal.

Iron is less reactive than carbon. Iron can be extracted from iron oxide by reducing the metal oxide with carbon.

potassium sodium calcium magnesium aluminium	**metals that are more reactive than carbon are extracted by** <u>**electrolysis**</u>
carbon zinc iron tin lead gold	**metals that are less reactive than carbon are extracted by reducing the metal oxide using** <u>**carbon**</u> **(or carbon monoxide)**

The solid raw materials

The solid raw materials in the blast furnace are:

- iron ore
- coke (which is a source of the element carbon)
- limestone (which reacts with impurities).

The main ore of iron is **haematite**. This ore contains the compound iron (III) oxide, Fe_2O_3.

What happens in the blast furnace?

1 Hot air is blasted into the furnace. The oxygen in the air reacts with the carbon in the coke to form carbon dioxide and release energy.

> carbon + oxygen → carbon dioxide
>
> $C_{(s)}$ + $O_{2(g)}$ → $CO_{2(g)}$

2 At the very high temperatures inside the blast furnace, carbon dioxide reacts with more carbon to form carbon monoxide.

> carbon dioxide + carbon → carbon monoxide
>
> $CO_{2(g)}$ + $C_{(s)}$ → $2CO_{(g)}$

3 The carbon monoxide reacts with iron oxide to form iron and carbon dioxide.

> carbon monoxide + iron oxide → iron + carbon dioxide
>
> $3CO_{(g)}$ + $Fe_2O_{3(s)}$ → $2Fe_{(l)}$ + $3CO_{2(g)}$

During this reaction:

- **the iron oxide is reduced to iron**
- **the carbon monoxide is oxidised to carbon dioxide.**

Due to the high temperatures in the blast furnace, the iron that is made is a liquid. This molten iron is dense and sinks to the bottom of the furnace where it can be removed.

 Iron ore is mainly reduced by the gas carbon monoxide.

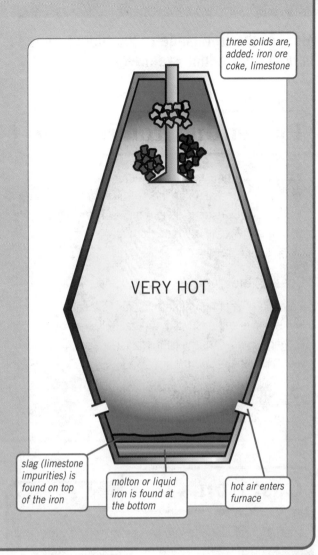

three solids are, added: iron ore coke, limestone

VERY HOT

slag (limestone impurities) is found on top of the iron

molton or liquid iron is found at the bottom

hot air enters furnace

Removing impurities in the blast furnace

Haematite (iron ore) contains many impurities; most commonly it contains substantial amounts of silicon dioxide (silica). Limestone is added to the blast furnace because it reacts with these silica impurities to form **slag**. Slag has a low density and so it floats to the top of the iron ore where it can be removed. The slag can be used in road building and in the manufacture of fertilisers.

1 Which element is so unreactive that it can be found uncombined?

2 Which method of extraction can be used for metals that are less reactive than carbon?

3 Which method of extraction can be used for metals that are more reactive than carbon?

4 What is the name of the main ore of iron?

5 What are the three solid raw materials added to the blast furnace?

6 What is the other raw material used in the blast furnace?

7 Which gas actually reduces iron oxide to iron?

8 Why does iron sink to the bottom of the furnace?

9 What is the name of the substance formed when limestone reacts with silica?

10 How can this substance be used?

Iron and steel

Most of the iron made in the blast furnace is used to produce steel.

Preventing iron rusting

Iron corrodes or 'rusts' faster than most transition metals. Rusting requires the presence of both oxygen and water. If we completely remove either of these two chemicals, we can stop the iron from rusting. This can be done in several ways.

Coating the iron

Painting or coating iron in plastic or oil can stop **oxygen and water** from reaching the metal and prevent it rusting. As soon as the coating is damaged, however, the iron will start to rust.

Sacrificial protection

Sacrificial protection involves a different approach.

We can stop iron from rusting by placing it in contact with a more reactive metal like **zinc** or **magnesium**. The iron is protected because the more reactive metal reacts instead of the iron. For this reason, the method is called sacrificial protection. Expensive objects made from iron, such as speedboat engines, are protected in this way.

Alloying the metal

Mixing iron with other metals and carbon to form alloys, such as stainless steel, will also protect the metal.

Cast iron

The iron that is made in a blast furnace contains large amounts of the element carbon. If this iron is allowed to cool down and solidify, it forms cast iron. Cast iron contains about 96% pure iron and can be used to make objects like drain covers. It:

■ is hard
■ is strong
■ does not rust.

Cast iron does have one notable disadvantage. It is brittle and can crack easily.

Drain covers need to be strong and must not rust. They are made from cast iron

Wrought iron

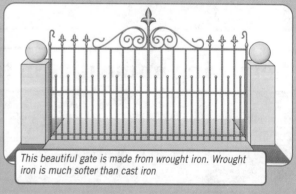

This beautiful gate is made from wrought iron. Wrought iron is much softer than cast iron

Wrought iron is made by removing the impurities from cast iron. Wrought iron is much softer than cast iron and can be used to make objects like gates.

Wrought iron is softer than cast iron because of its structure. Wrought iron is made from almost pure iron. This means that the iron atoms form a **very regular arrangement**. The layers of iron atoms are able to slip easily over each other. This makes wrought iron soft and easy to shape.

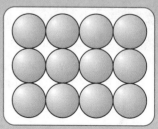

Steel

Most iron is made into steel. In fact, most of the metal objects that we use today are made from steel. To make steel:

- Any carbon impurities must first be removed from the iron, to produce pure iron.
- Other metals and carefully controlled amounts of the non-metal element carbon are added to the iron.

Steel is much harder than wrought iron because it consists of atoms of different elements. These atoms are different sizes. This means that the atoms in steel cannot pack together to form regular structure. This irregular structure makes it **very difficult for layers of** **atoms to slide** over each other and makes the steel very hard.

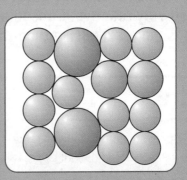

Designer steels

By carefully controlling the amount of carbon that is added to steel, scientists can produce metal that has exactly the right properties for each particular job.

Low carbon steels are:

- soft
- easy to shape.

Objects such as car bodies are made from low carbon steels.

Medium carbon steels are:

- harder
- stronger
- less easy to shape.

Objects such as hammers are made from medium carbon steels.

High carbon steels are:

- hard
- strong
- brittle
- hard to shape.

Objects such as razor blades are made from high carbon steels.

We can also alloy iron with other metals to form different types of steel.

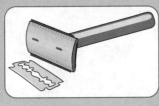

Stainless steel

Stainless steel is a very widely used **alloy**. It consists of:

- 70% iron
- 20% chromium
- 10% nickel.

Stainless steel is extremely resistant to corrosion.

QUICK TEST

1. What is the main use of iron?
2. What must be present for iron to rust?
3. How does oiling an iron object stop it from rusting?
4. Name a metal that could be used in sacrificial protection to stop iron rusting.
5. What is the main impurity in cast iron?
6. Give four properties of cast iron.
7. What is the name given to very pure iron?
8. Why is pure iron soft?
9. Which non-metal element is used to make steel?
10. Which metals can be alloyed to form stainless steel?

Aluminium

Aluminium is abundant in the Earth's crust, but it is also very reactive. Consequently, aluminium is more expensive than iron.

Aluminium alloys are strong and lightweight

Bauxite

The main ore of aluminium is called **bauxite**. Bauxite contains the compound aluminium oxide, Al_2O_3. Unfortunately, bauxite is often found in environmentally sensitive areas such as the Amazonian rainforests. Extracting bauxite from these places brings jobs and money to the area, but can also scar the landscape and harm local wildlife. New roads can damage the areas around the mines and local people can be displaced by the development.

Recycling aluminium

One way to protect the areas where bauxite is found is for people to simply **recycle** their old aluminium cans. Recycling has many advantages. It means that:

■ we will not have to extract so much bauxite

■ landfill sites will not be filled up with discarded aluminium cans

■ much less energy is used than when we extract aluminium straight from its ore.

Properties of aluminium

Although pure aluminium is quite soft, when it is alloyed with other metals it becomes much stronger. **Aluminium alloys combine high strength with low density.** This makes aluminium a very useful metal for producing objects like aeroplanes and mountain bikes.

Aluminium is quite a reactive metal and yet it is widely used to make drink cans. In fact, aluminium is much less reactive than its position in the reactivity series would suggest. This is because, when aluminium objects are made, their surfaces quickly react with oxygen to form a thin **layer of aluminium oxide**. This layer stops the aluminium metal from coming into contact with other chemicals and so prevents any further reaction. The layer of aluminium oxide means that it is quite safe for us to drink fizzy, acidic drinks from aluminium cans.

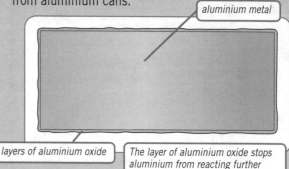

aluminium metal

layers of aluminium oxide

The layer of aluminium oxide stops aluminium from reacting further

The extraction of aluminium

Aluminium is more reactive than carbon and so it is extracted using electrolysis, even though this is a very expensive method. The main ore of aluminium is bauxite which contains aluminium oxide. For electrolysis to occur, the aluminium ions and oxide ions in bauxite must be able to move. This means that the bauxite has to be either heated until it melts or dissolved in something.

Bauxite has a very high melting point and heating the ore to this temperature is very expensive. Fortunately, another ore of aluminium called **cryolite** has a much lower melting point. First, the cryolite is heated up until it melts; then the bauxite is **dissolved** in the molten cryolite.

Electrolysis

Aluminium can now be extracted by electrolysis (using electricity).

1 By dissolving the aluminium oxide, both the aluminium, Al^{3+} and the oxide, O^{2-} ions can move.

2 During electrolysis the aluminium Al^{3+} ions are attracted to the negative electrode where they pick up electrons to form aluminium Al atoms. The aluminium metal collects at the bottom of the cell where it can be gathered.

> aluminium ions + electrons → aluminium atoms
> Al^{3+} + $3e^-$ → Al

3 The oxide, O^{2-} ions are attracted to the positive electrode where they deposit electrons to form oxygen molecules.

> oxide ions − electrons → oxygen molecules
> $2O^{2-}$ − $4e^-$ → O_2

4 The oxygen that forms at the positive electrode readily reacts with the carbon, graphite electrode to form carbon dioxide. The electrodes, therefore, must be replaced periodically.

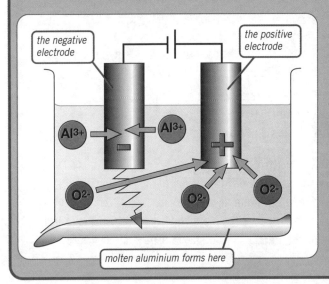

the negative electrode

the positive electrode

molten aluminium forms here

Oxidation and reduction

In the electrolysis of aluminium oxide the following occurs:

- **Aluminium ions are reduced to aluminium atoms.**
- **Oxide ions are oxidised to oxygen molecules.**

Reduction reactions happen when a substance gains electrons. Here, each aluminium ion gains three electrons to form an aluminium atom.

Oxidation reactions occur when a substance loses electrons. Here, two oxide ions both lose two electrons to form an oxygen molecule.

Reduction and oxidation reactions must always occur together and so are sometimes referred to as **redox** reactions.

Oxidation and reduction can be remembered using the mnemonic 'OIL RIG', which stands for:
Oxidation
Is
Loss
Reduction
Is
Gain
(of electrons)

QUICK TEST

1. Name the main ore of aluminium.
2. Give two properties of pure aluminium.
3. What is a mixture of metals called?
4. Why is aluminium less reactive than expected?
5. What is the formula of aluminium oxide?
6. What is the name of the method used to extract aluminium from its ore?
7. During the electrolysis of aluminium oxide which ions are oxidised?
8. During the electrolysis of aluminium oxide which ions are reduced?
9. What are the electrodes made from?
10. Why should the electrodes be periodically replaced?

Titanium

Despite being abundant in the Earth's crust, *titanium* is an expensive metal. This is because it is difficult to extract titanium from its ore.

The F22 fighter is made from a titanium alloy

Properties of titanium

Titanium has some very special properties.
Titanium:

- is very strong when alloyed with other metals
- has a very low density
- is easy to shape
- has a very high melting point
- is very resistant to corrosion.

Titanium appears to be unreactive, because the surface of titanium objects quickly reacts with oxygen to form a **layer of titanium dioxide**. This layer prevents any further reaction taking place.

Uses of titanium

Titanium's properties mean that this metal is very useful. Titanium alloys are used to make:

- replacement hip and elbow joints
- aircraft
- rockets and missiles.

Titanium ore

The main ore of titanium is **rutile**. Rutile contains the compound **titanium dioxide**, TiO_2. Rutile is a very hard mineral that is resistant to weathering and is found mixed among sand on certain beaches.

Extraction of titanium

Titanium is more reactive than carbon and so cannot be extracted simply by heating titanium dioxide with carbon. The extraction of titanium is quite a complicated process.

- First the titanium dioxide is converted to **titanium chloride**.
- Then the titanium chloride is reacted with **molten magnesium**. Magnesium is more reactive than titanium and a chemical reaction takes place in which titanium is displaced.

titanium chloride + magnesium → titanium + magnesium chloride

$$TiCl_4 + 2Mg \rightarrow Ti + 2MgCl_2$$

This reaction is carried out in a vacuum to stop the titanium from reacting with oxygen in the air to form titanium dioxide.

Smart alloys 1

Smart alloys are new materials with amazing properties. One famous example of a smart alloy is nitinol. Nitinol is an alloy of nickel and titanium.

Smart alloys have a shape memory. When a force is applied to a smart alloy it stretches. When a smart alloy is heated up, however, it returns to its original shape.

Why do smart alloys have a shape memory?

Smart alloys appear to have a shape memory because they are able to exist in **two solid forms**. A temperature change of 10-20°C is enough to cause smart alloys to change forms.

At low temperatures, smart alloys exist in their low-temperature form.

If a force is applied to the alloy, it can be distorted to form the low-temperature, deformed form of the alloy. When the alloy is heated, it changes to the higher temperature form.

In smart alloys, the low-temperature form and the high-temperature form are the same shape and size and so, when they are heated, smart alloys appear to have a shape memory.

Smart alloys 2

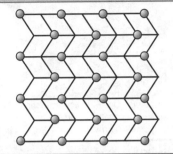

At low temperatures, smart alloys exist in their low temperature form

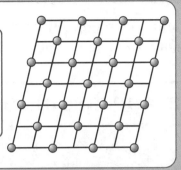

If a force is applied to the alloy it can be deformed to form the low-temperature, deformed form of the alloy

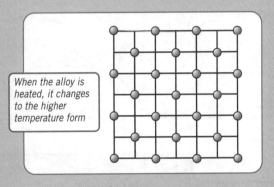

When the alloy is heated, it changes to the higher temperature form

Nano-materials

Scientists are currently researching the properties of new nano-materials. These substances contain **just a few hundred** atoms and vary in size from 1 nm to 100 nm. They have a very high surface area to volume ratio.

Scientists hope that this property of nano-molecules will allow them to be used in exciting ways such as:

■ in new computers
■ as better catalysts.

QUICK TEST

1. How can titanium be made stronger?
2. Why does titanium appear to be unreactive?
3. How is titanium used inside the human body?
4. What is the main ore of titanium?
5. What is the chemical name of the main ore of titanium?
6. Where is titanium ore collected?
7. Why is titanium not extracted from its ore by using carbon?
8. Which metal is more reactive, titanium or magnesium?
9. Give the word equation for the reaction between titanium chloride and magnesium.
10. Which metals are used to produce the smart alloy nitinol?

Copper

Copper is an unreactive metal that has been known since ancient times.

This saucepan is made from copper. Copper is a good thermal conductor and does not contaminate the food that is being cooked

Properties of copper

Copper has some very special properties. Copper is:

- a good thermal conductor
- a good electrical conductor
- easy to shape
- very unreactive
- very resistant to corrosion.

In fact, the metal copper is so unreactive that it does not even react with water.

Uses of copper

Copper's properties mean that it is a very useful metal. Copper is used to make:

- water pipes
- saucepans
- electrical wires.

Copper ore

Copper has several ores, but as copper has been known for a long time, the richest supplies of ores have been exhausted. We now extract copper from rocks that do not contain large amounts of the metal. This means that **a lot of rock has to be quarried** in order to extract enough copper. As a consequence, copper mines tend to be very large and can cause significant damage to the local area. Today, the most important copper ores are **chalcopyrite** and **chalcosine**.

Extraction of copper

Copper is extracted from its ores in a series of steps.

1 First the rocks containing copper are broken down into small pieces.

2 These pieces of rock are then mixed with water and detergent. The copper-rich particles float to the top and are removed. The copper is mainly found in the compound, copper sulphide.

3 The **copper sulphide is heated in air to form copper oxide and sulphur dioxide**.

> copper sulphide + oxygen → copper oxide + sulphur dioxide

4 Finally, the **copper oxide is reacted with more copper sulphide to form copper and sulphur dioxide**.

> copper oxide + copper sulphide → copper + sulphur dioxide

Copper produced in this way is not, however, pure enough for many uses.

Scientists, therefore, are developing ways to exploit copper from 'low-grade' ores, which contain copper at lower concentrations than would normally be economically worthwhile. The idea is to leach copper out of the ores to form a solution, then extract the copper from the solution using electrolysis.

Copper can be extracted from its ore chalcopyrite

Purification of copper

Copper has to be purified before it can be used for certain applications, such as in high specification wiring. Copper is purified using electrolysis.

💡 *Electrolysis involves passing an electrical current through a molten ionic substance or dissolved ionic substance to break down the substance into simpler parts.*

- During the electrolysis of copper, the impure copper metal is used as the positive electrode.
- At the positive electrode, the copper atoms give up electrons to form copper ions.

> copper atoms – electrons → copper ions
> Cu – $2e^-$ → Cu^{2+}

- As the positive electrode dissolves away, any impurities fall to the bottom of the cell to form sludge.
- Copper ions in the solution are attracted towards the negative electrode.

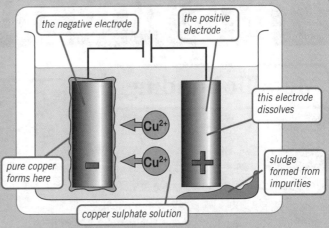

the negative electrode

the positive electrode

this electrode dissolves

pure copper forms here

sludge formed from impurities

copper sulphate solution

- At the negative electrode, the copper ions gain electrons to form copper atoms.

> copper ions + electrons → copper atoms
> Cu^{2+} + $2e^-$ → Cu

- The positive electrode gets smaller while the negative electrode gets bigger. In addition, the negative electrode is covered in very pure copper.

Copper alloys

Pure copper is too soft for many uses. In pure copper, the atoms are all the same size and so they form a regular arrangement. Copper is soft because the layers of atoms can pass over each other easily.

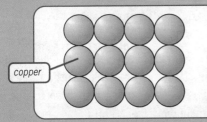

copper

Copper is often mixed with other metals to form alloys.

Bronze is made by mixing copper and tin. It is much harder than either copper or tin and consists of different sized atoms, which means that the atoms cannot pack together to form a regular structure. Bronze is hard because the layers of atoms cannot pass over each other easily.

Historically, the invention of bronze was a major

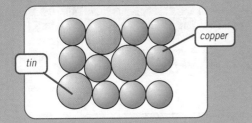

copper

tin

advance: it was used to make new, stronger tools and weapons.

Brass is made by mixing copper and zinc and has several useful properties. It is a good electrical conductor and does not tarnish easily. Brass is often used to make musical instruments.

QUICK TEST

1. Name two copper ores.
2. Which gas is produced when copper sulphide is heated in the air?
3. How may scientists obtain copper in the future?
4. What method is used to purify copper?
5. Give the symbol equation for the reaction that takes place at the positive electrode during the purification of copper.
6. Give the symbol equation for the reaction that takes place at the negative electrode during the purification of copper.
7. If you wanted to coat a metal object with copper, which electrode should you attach it to?
8. What name is used to describe a mixture of metals?
9. Which metals are used to make bronze?
10. Which metals are used to make brass?

Transition metals

Metallic bonding

Metals have a giant structure. In metals, the electrons in the highest energy shells (the outer electrons) are not bound to a single atom, but are free to move through the whole structure. This means that metals consist of positive metal ions surrounded by a sea of negative electrons. **Metallic bonding is the attraction between these ions and the electrons.**

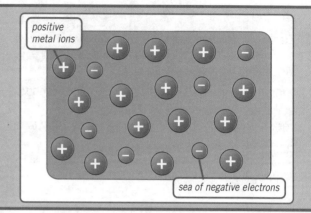

positive metal ions

sea of negative electrons

Properties of metals

Metallic bonding means that metals have several, very useful properties.

- The free electrons mean that metals are **good electrical conductors**.
- The free electrons also mean that metals are **good thermal conductors**.
- The strong attraction between the metal ions and the electrons means that metals can be drawn into **wires** as the ions slide over each other.
- Metals can also be **hammered into shape**.

The transition metals are found in the middle section of the periodic table. Copper, iron and nickel are examples of very useful transition metals. All transition metals have characteristic properties. They have:

- **high melting points** (except for mercury which is a liquid at room temperature)
- **high density**
- coloured compounds.

They are also strong, tough and hard wearing. All transition metals are much less reactive than Group 1 metals. They react much less vigorously with oxygen and water.

Many transition metals can **form ions with different charges**. This makes transition metals useful catalysts in many reactions.

Transition metals all have similar properties because of their electron structure. The first row of transition elements (from scandium to zinc) all behave in a very similar way. This is because we are actually filling a lower energy electron shell, not the outer electron shell, which determines how the atoms react.

Normally the third shell can hold up to eight electrons. However, once two electrons have been placed into the fourth shell, this structure changes and the third shell can hold up to 18 electrons. The transition metals all behave in a similar way to each other because their outer shell contains two electrons.

	Group																	
	1	2											3	4	5	6	7	0
1	H Hydrogen																	He Helium
2	Li Lithium	Be Beryllium											B Boron	C Carbon	N Nitrogen	O Oxygen	F Fluorine	Ne Neon
3	Na Sodium	Mg Magnesium											Al Aluminium	Si Silicon	P Phosphorous	S Sulphur	Cl Chlorine	Ar Argon
4	K Potassium	Ca Calcium	Sc Scandium	Ti Titanium	V Vanadium	Cr Chromium	Mn Manganese	Fe Iron	Co Cobalt	Ni Nickel	Cu Copper	Zn Zinc	Ga Gallium	Ge Germanium	As Arsenic	Se Selenium	Br Bromine	Kr Krypton
5	Rb Rubidium	Sr Strontium	Y Yttrium	Zr Zirconium	Nb Niobium	Mo Molybdenum	Tc Technetium	Ru Ruthenium	Rh Rhodium	Pd Palladium	Ag Silver	Cd Cadmium	In Indium	Sn Tin	Sb Antimony	Te Tellurium	I Iodine	Xe Xenon
6	Cs Caesium	Ba Barium	La Lanthanum	Hf Hafnium	Ta Tantalum	W Tungsten	Re Rhenium	Os Osmium	Ir Iridium	Pt Platinum	Au Gold	Hg Mercury	Tl Thallium	Pb Lead	Bi Bismuth	Po Polonium	At Astatine	Rn Radon
7	Fr Francium	Ra Radium	Ac Actinium															

Period

Copper

- Copper is a good electrical and thermal conductor.
- It can be easily bent into new shapes and does not corrode.
- Copper is widely used in electrical wiring.
- It is also used to make water pipes.

Nickel

- Nickel is hard, shiny and dense.
- It is widely used to make coins.
- Nickel is used as a catalyst in the manufacture of margarine.

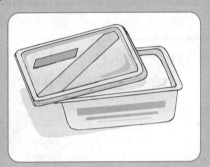

Iron

- Iron made in the blast furnace is strong but brittle.
- Iron is often made into steel.
- Steel is strong and cheap and is used in vast quantities. However, it is also heavy and may rust.
- Iron and steel are useful structural materials. They are used to make buildings, bridges, ships, cars and trains.
- Iron is used as a catalyst in the Haber process.

Metal alloys

Alloys are made by mixing metals together.
Occasionally, alloys can be made by mixing metals with non-metals.

Common alloys include:

- amalgams, which are mainly mercury
- brass, which is made from copper and zinc
- bronze, which is made from copper and tin
- solder, which is made from lead and tin
- steel, which is mainly iron.

QUICK TEST

1. Why are metals able to conduct heat and electricity?
2. In which part of the periodic table are the transition metals found?
3. What are the characteristics of transition metals?
4. Why is copper used for electrical wiring?
5. Why is copper used for water pipes?
6. Why is iron made into steel?
7. Which items can be made from steel?
8. In which process is iron used as a catalyst?
9. Which items can be made from nickel?
10. Nickel is used as a catalyst for the manufacture of which foodstuff?

Noble gases

The noble gases are very unreactive. They are sometimes described as being 'inert' because they do not react. This is because they have a full, stable outer shell of electrons.

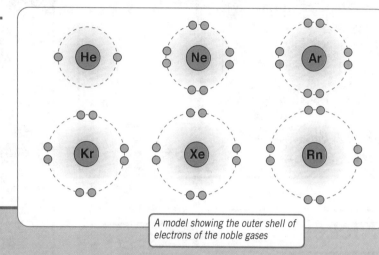

A model showing the outer shell of electrons of the noble gases

Characteristics of noble gases

- The noble gases are found on the far right-hand side of the periodic table.
- The noble gases are all colourless.

- They are **monatomic gases**. This means that they exist as single atoms rather than as diatomic molecules as other gases do.

Why do melting and boiling points increase down the group?

- Melting and boiling points increase as you go down the group.
- The atoms get larger and have more electrons.
- This means that the strength of the attraction between atoms increases.
- As the **attraction between atoms gets stronger**, it takes more energy to overcome these forces.
- As a result, noble gases will melt and boil at higher temperatures.

5	6	7	0
			He Helium
O Oxygen	**F** Fluorine	**Ne** Neon	
S Sulphur	**Cl** Chlorine	**Ar** Argon	
Se Selenium	**Br** Bromine	**Kr** Krypton	
Te Tellurium	**I** Iodine	**Xe** Xenon	
Po Polonium	**At** Astatine	**Rn** Radon	

Why are noble gases so unreactive?

When atoms react, they share, gain or lose electrons to obtain a full outer shell of electrons. **Noble gases already have a full and stable outer shell and so they do not react**. They are useful to us precisely because they do not react.

Uses of the noble gases

Helium

Helium is used in balloons and in airships because it is less dense than air.

It is not flammable. (Early airships used hydrogen, which is flammable, and this caused problems.)

Neon

Neon is used in electrical discharge tubes in advertising signs.

Radon

Radon is a noble gas. It is chemically unreactive but it is radioactive. Home owners in some parts of the country such as Cornwall and Northamptonshire use these devices to monitor radon levels.

Argon

Argon is used in filament light bulbs.

The hot filament is surrounded by argon. This stops the filament from burning away and breaking the bulb.

Krypton

Krypton is used in lasers.

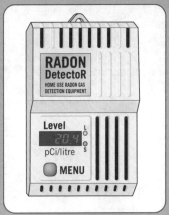

QUICK TEST

1. Why are the noble gases so unreactive?
2. What is the trend in boiling point down the group?
3. Draw the (outer shell) electron shell of helium.
4. Draw the (outer shell) electron shell of argon.
5. What does monatomic mean?
6. What is helium used for?
7. Why is helium so useful?
8. What is neon used for?
9. What is argon used for?
10. What is krypton used for?

Chemical tests

In this subject, we often wish to identify the chemical present.

Gas tests

Carbon dioxide

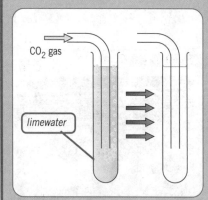

CO₂ gas

limewater

What do you do?

The gas is bubbled through limewater.

What happens?

The limewater turns cloudy.

Carbonates react with acids to produce carbon dioxide.

Hydrogen

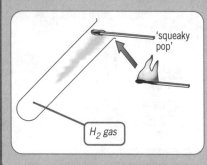

'squeaky pop'

H₂ gas

What do you do?

A lighted splint is placed nearby.

What happens?

The hydrogen burns with a squeaky pop.

Chlorine

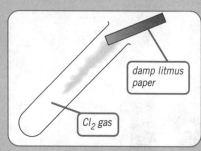

damp litmus paper

Cl₂ gas

What do you do?

Place damp litmus paper in the gas.

What happens?

The litmus paper is bleached.

Oxygen

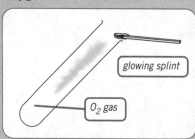

glowing splint

O₂ gas

What do you do?

A glowing splint is placed in the gas.

What happens?

The splint relights.

Ammonia

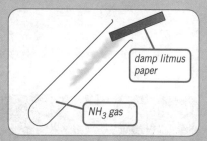

damp litmus paper

NH₃ gas

What do you do?

Place damp red litmus paper in the gas.

What happens?

The red litmus paper turns blue.

Sodium hydroxide solution reacts with ammonium ions to form ammonia.

Nitrate ions are reduced by aluminium powder and sodium hydroxide to form ammonia.

Testing for alkenes

Alkenes are unsaturated hydrocarbons.

What do you do?

Add bromine water.

What happens?

The orange-brown bromine water becomes colourless.

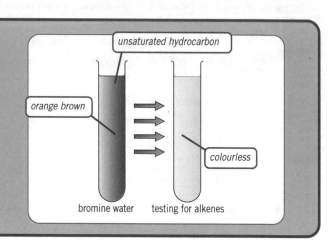

unsaturated hydrocarbon

orange brown

colourless

bromine water   testing for alkenes

Testing for carbonates

Carbonates react with acids to form carbon dioxide. When copper carbonate is heated, it decomposes to form copper oxide and carbon dioxide. This can be identified by a distinctive colour change: **copper carbonate is green** and **copper oxide is black**.

When zinc carbonate is heated it decomposes to form zinc oxide and carbon dioxide. This can also be identified by a distinctive colour change: **zinc carbonate is white; while zinc oxide is yellow when hot but, as it cools, it turns white**.

Hydroxide tests

We can identify other metals by adding sodium hydroxide solution to solutions of the salt. If the unknown metal forms an **insoluble precipitate**, we can use the colour of the precipitate to identify the metal present:

- aluminium – white precipitate which dissolves in excess sodium hydroxide
- calcium – white precipitate
- magnesium – white precipitate

- copper (II) – pale blue precipitate
- iron (II) – green precipitate
- iron (III) – brown precipitate.

Flame tests

Flame tests can be used to identify some metals present in salts.

What do you do?

1 Clean a flame test wire by placing it into the hottest part of a Bunsen flame.
2 Dip the end of the wire into water and then into the salt sample.
3 Hold the salt sample in the hottest part of the flame and observe the colour seen.

What happens?

The flame alters colour according to the salt:

- lithium - red
- sodium - orange
- potassium - lilac
- calcium - brick red
- barium - apple green.

Modern instrumental methods

Modern instrumental techniques can be used to **detect and identify chemicals**. These modern techniques have many advantages. They are:

- accurate
- sensitive
- fast
- can be used when there are only very small samples available.

Some techniques, such as atomic absorption spectroscopy, are used to identify elements.

Other techniques are used to identify compounds. These include:

- infrared spectroscopy
- ultraviolet spectroscopy
- nuclear magnetic spectroscopy
- gas-liquid chromatography.

Mass spectroscopy can be used to identify elements or compounds.

QUICK TEST

1 What is the test for carbon dioxide?
2 What is the test for chlorine?
3 What is the test for ammonia?
4 What is the test for unsaturated hydrocarbons?
5 What is the gas produced when carbonates react with acid?
6 What is the colour of copper carbonate?
7 During a flame test what colour is given by a potassium salt?
8 During a flame test what colour is given by a barium salt?
9 What colour precipitate is formed when a solution of a magnesium salt reacts with sodium hydroxide?
10 What colour precipitate is formed when a solution of a copper (II) salt reacts with sodium hydroxide?

Practice questions

Use the questions to test your progress. Check your answers on page 126.

1. This table is about limestone and some of the substances that can be made from limestone.

Substance	Information about the substance
A	is made when limestone is heated with silica and soda.
B	is made when water is added to calcium oxide.
C	is a rock that contains large amounts of calcium carbonate.
D	is formed when calcium carbonate is heated.

a) What is the name of substance C?..

b) What is the chemical name of substance D?...

c) What is the formula of substance B?..

d) What is the name of substance A? ....

2. Atoms can join together to form molecules. Here are four diagrams of molecules.

a) $H-\overset{\displaystyle H}{\underset{\displaystyle H}{C}}-H$ b) $H-\overset{\displaystyle H}{\underset{\displaystyle H}{C}}-\overset{\displaystyle H}{\underset{\displaystyle H}{C}}-H$ c) $\overset{H}{\underset{H}{}}C=C\overset{H}{\underset{H}{}}$ d) $H-\overset{\displaystyle H}{\underset{\displaystyle H}{C}}-\overset{\displaystyle H}{\underset{\displaystyle}{C}}=C\overset{H}{\underset{H}{}}$

a) What is the formula of molecule A?..

b) What is the name of molecule B?...

c) What family of organic compounds do molecules A and B belong to? ....

d) What is the formula of molecule C?..

e) What is the name of molecule D?...

f) What family of organic compounds do molecules C and D belong to?.............................

3. Crude oil can be separated into fractions.

a) What is the name of the process used to separate crude oil into fractions? ....

b) Molecules found in the diesel oil fraction contain about 20 carbon atoms. Molecules in the petrol fraction contain about eight carbon atoms. Tick one box to show how petrol and diesel molecules compare.
Compared with diesel molecules, petrol molecules:

are more flammable ☐   are more viscous ☐   have a higher boiling point ☐
have more carbon atoms ☐

c) Some long hydrocarbon molecules can be split into smaller, more useful molecules. What is the name of the process used to break up long hydrocarbon molecules into shorter, more useful hydrocarbons?

....

4. Which of these diagrams represents a molecule of butane, C_4H_{10}?

```
   H  H  H              H  H  H  H            H  H  H  H             H   H-C-H
   |  |  |              |  |  |  |            |  |  |  |             |   |
H -C -C -C -H        H -C -C -C -C -H        C =C -C -C -H        H -C -C =C
   |  |  |              |  |  |  |            |     |  |             |   |   |
   H  H  H              H  H  H  H            H     H  H             H   H   H
```

5. a) What is the name given to a mixture of metals? ....

....

b) Which metals are mixed together to form stainless steel? ....

....

c) Which non-metal element is often added to steel to make it harder? ....

6. a) Sketch the arrangement of atoms in pure titanium.

b) Sketch the arrangement of atoms in a titanium alloy.

c) Explain why titanium alloy is stronger than pure titanium. ....

....

....

7. Iron is produced in the blast furnace. Place these statements in order to show how iron is produced.
   a) Carbon dioxide reacts with carbon to form carbon monoxide.
   b) The iron is dense and sinks to the bottom of the furnace where it can be removed.
   c) Carbon reacts with oxygen to form carbon dioxide.
   d) The carbon monoxide reacts with iron oxide to form iron and carbon dioxide.

....

8. This table shows the names of four different salts.

Name of salt
zinc carbonate
potassium chloride
lithium chloride
copper carbonate

a) During a flame test, which salt produces a red colour?

....

b) Which salt turns black on heating?

....

c) Which white salt turns yellow on heating and then, when cooled, turns white again?

....

d) During a flame test, which salt produces a lilac colour?

....

9. a) Which gas relights a glowing splint?
   b) Which gas bleaches damp litmus paper?
   c) Which gas burns with a squeaky pop?
   d) Which gas turns damp red litmus blue?

Energy

Many devices take in one form of energy and transform it into another. It is important that we know how efficiently they do this so that we can choose between them and where possible try to improve them.

Different forms of energy

The table below is a reminder of the different forms of energy.

Types of energy	Sources
heat or thermal energy	hot objects, such as fires
light energy	the Sun, light bulbs, lamps, etc.
sound energy	loudspeakers, vibrating objects
electrical energy	available every time a current flows
chemical energy	food, fuels and batteries
kinetic energy (the energy an object has because it is moving)	flowing water, wind, etc.
elastic or strain potential energy	objects such as springs and rubber bands that are stretched, twisted or bent
gravitational potential energy	objects that have a high position and are able to fall
nuclear energy	reactions in the centre, or nucleus, of an atom

Energy transfers 1

Energy cannot be created or destroyed. When energy is used **it does not disappear**. It is **transferred into other forms** of energy.

A **light bulb** transfers **electrical energy** into **heat and light energy**.

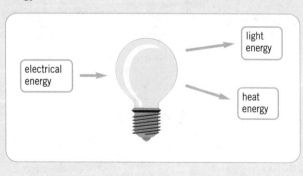

The **motor** inside this train transfers **electrical energy** into **kinetic energy**.

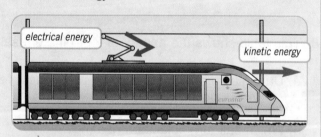

A **loudspeaker** transfers **electrical energy** into **sound energy**.

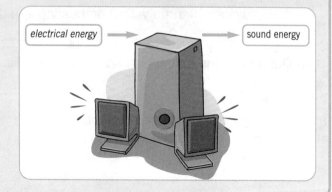

Energy transfers 2

Other examples of energy changes are given in the table below.

Energy in	Energy changer	Energy out
chemical (food)	animal	heat, kinetic, chemical
light	solar cell	electrical
kinetic	wind turbine	electrical
strain potential energy	bow and arrow	kinetic energy
chemical	battery	electrical
electrical	battery charger	chemical
sound	microphone	electrical
kinetic energy	generator	electrical
gravitational potential energy	falling object	kinetic energy
strain potential energy	clockwork car	kinetic energy

Efficiency

Usually, when an energy transfer takes place, only part of the energy is transformed into something useful. The remainder is wasted.

Example 1

The bulb (above) is not 100% efficient. Not all of the energy is transferred into light; some of it is transferred into heat.

To calculate the efficiency of a transfer we use the equation:

$$\text{Efficiency} = \frac{\text{useful energy output}}{\text{total energy input}} \times 100\%$$

In this case, 200 J of electrical energy enters the bulb, of which 8 J is transferred into light energy and 192 J is transferred into heat.

$$\text{Efficiency} = \frac{\text{useful energy output}}{\text{total energy input}} \times 100\%$$

The efficiency of the bulb $= \frac{8\text{ J}}{200\text{ J}} \times 100\% = 4\%$.

Example 2

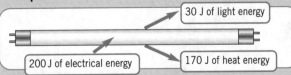

$$\text{Efficiency} = \frac{\text{useful energy output}}{\text{total energy input}} \times 100\%$$

The efficiency of the light $= \frac{30\text{ J}}{200\text{ J}} \times 100\% = 15\%$.

We can see from these figures that a fluorescent light is more efficient than a traditional light bulb.

Example 3

Compact fluorescent light bulbs like the one above are even more efficient.

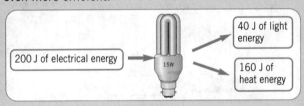

$$\text{Efficiency} = \frac{\text{useful energy output}}{\text{total energy input}} \times 100\%$$

The efficiency of the bulb $= \frac{40\text{ J}}{200\text{ J}} \times 100\% = 20\%$.

In nearly all devices, wasted energy is eventually transferred to the surroundings, which then become warmer.

An efficient device saves you money and helps protect the environment by reducing your energy consumption. An inefficient device wastes energy and helps deplete our energy resources.

QUICK TEST

1 Name five different types of energy.
2 Name three devices that transfer electrical energy.
3 What kind of energy does a crate gain as it is lifted by an electric hoist?
4 Write down the energy transfer that takes place when using a hairdryer.
5 How much energy is lost during an energy transfer?

Generating electricity

Electricity is one of the most convenient forms of energy. It is easily converted into other forms of energy and it can be transferred across large distances.

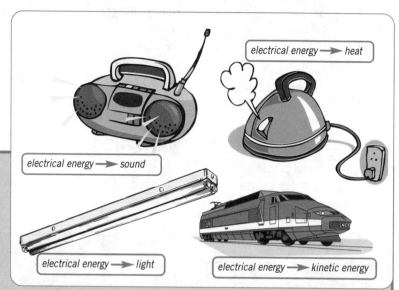

electrical energy ➝ heat

electrical energy ➝ sound

electrical energy ➝ light

electrical energy ➝ kinetic energy

Power stations

Most of the electrical energy we use at home is generated at **power stations**. There are several different types of power station including those that use **coal, oil or gas as their source of energy** (fuel).

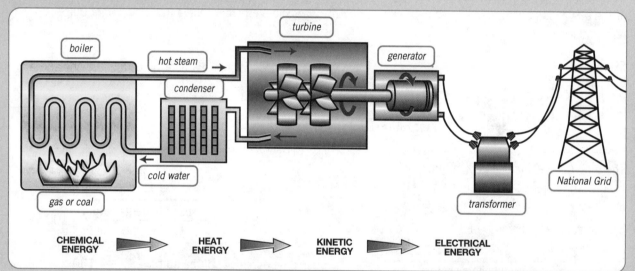

boiler

hot steam

condenser

turbine

generator

cold water

gas or coal

transformer

National Grid

| CHEMICAL ENERGY | ➡ | HEAT ENERGY | ➡ | KINETIC ENERGY | ➡ | ELECTRICAL ENERGY |

- The fuel is burned to release its **chemical energy**.
- The **heat energy released** is used to heat water and turn it into steam.
- The steam **turns turbines**.
- The turbines **turn large generators**.
- The **generators produce electrical energy**.

- Before entering the National Grid, the electrical energy passes through a **transformer**, which increases its voltage and decreases the current. These changes **reduce the energy losses in the cables and wires**.
- The electrical energy is carried to our homes through the **National Grid**.

Fossil fuels

Coal, oil and gas are called **fossil fuels**. They are **concentrated sources** of energy.

Fossil fuels are formed from **plants and animals** that died over 100 million years ago. Having died, they were **covered with many layers of mud and earth**. The resulting

large pressures and high temperatures changed them into fossil fuels. Because they take **millions of years to form**, these fuels are called **non-renewable fuels**. Once they have been used up they **cannot be replaced**.

The problems with fossil fuels

The problems with fossil fuels

- When fossil fuels are burned, they produce **carbon dioxide**. Increasing the amount of carbon dioxide in the atmosphere will cause the temperature of the Earth and its atmosphere to rise. **This is called the greenhouse effect and could lead to drastic changes in climate, possibly resulting in flooding and drought.**
- When coal and oil are burned they produce gases that cause acid rain.
- **Environmental problems** are created by **mining** and **spillage of oil during transport.**
- We are using fossil fuels up very quickly and will soon have to find other sources of energy, but we need to start looking now.

The solutions

We need to slow down the rate at which we are using fossil fuels, so that they will last longer. There are several ways in which we can do this, for example by:

- **reducing petrol consumption** by driving smaller cars, using public transport, walking or cycling and by developing more efficient car engines
- **improving the insulation** of our homes and factories so less energy is wasted heating them
- **increasing the public's awareness** of how they are wasting energy so that they turn off lights and turn down heating where possible.

We need to use other sources of energy. **Renewable sources of energy**, such as wind, waves, tidal, solar, geothermal, biomass and hydroelectric, **need to be developed**. Each of these sources has some advantages and disadvantages.

In the UK, some of our electricity is generated by nuclear power stations. These stations have the advantage of producing electrical energy without emitting greenhouse or other polluting gases and the actual cost of producing electricity is very low. There are, however, several very serious disadvantages which need to be considered:

- The building and decommissioning (i.e. taking out of use and demolishing) of nuclear power stations is very expensive.
- Nuclear waste material will remain dangerously radioactive for thousands of years.
- There is always the danger that radioactive material may leak into the atmosphere.
- There is the risk of a nuclear explosion.

> *It is important to realise that our society depends heavily upon electricity and that the factors which affect the decisions concerning the sources of energy we use to generate it are political as well as economic. They are also crucial to the well-being of our planet.*

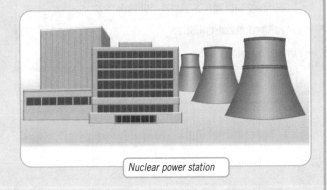

Nuclear power station

QUICK TEST

1. Name three fossil fuels.
2. What gas causes the greenhouse effect?
3. When burned, which fossil fuels cause most acid rain?
4. Name one type of environmental damage that might be caused as a result of using fossil fuels in our power stations.
5. Why are fossil fuels called non-renewable sources of energy?
6. Suggest two ways in which we could make fossil fuels last longer.

Renewable sources of energy

Unlike fossil fuels, there are some sources of energy that will not run out. They are continually being replaced. These are called *renewable sources of energy*. Each of these sources has advantages and disadvantages to their use. These should be considered carefully before any choice is made.

Wind power

The **kinetic energy of the wind** is used to drive turbines and generators.

+ It is a **renewable** source of energy and therefore will not be exhausted

+ It requires **low level technology** and therefore can be used by developing countries

+ It produces **no atmospheric pollution**

− **Visual and noise pollution**

− **Limited to windy sites**

− **No wind means no energy**

Hydroelectricity

The **kinetic energy of flowing water** is used to drive turbines and generators.

+ **Renewable source**

+ Energy **can be stored** until required

+ **No atmospheric pollution**

− **High initial cost**

− **High cost to environment**, i.e. flooding, loss of habitat

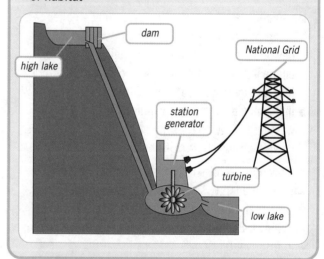

Wave power

The kinetic energy of the **rocking motion of the waves** is used to generate electricity.

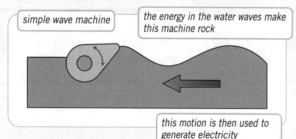

simple wave machine

the energy in the water waves make this machine rock

this motion is then used to generate electricity

+ **Renewable source**

+ **No atmospheric pollution**

+ **Useful for isolated islands**

− **High initial cost**

− **Visual pollution**

− **Poor energy capture**; large area of machines needed even for small energy return

Tidal power

At high tide, water is trapped behind a barrage or dam. When it is released at low tide, the **gravitational potential energy of the water** changes into kinetic energy, which then drives turbines and generates electricity.

+ **Renewable source**

+ **Reliable** – always two tides per day

+ **No atmospheric pollution**

+ **Low running costs**

− **High initial cost**

− **Possible damage to environment**, e.g. flooding

− **Obstacle to water transport**

Geothermal

In regions where the Earth's crust is thin, hot rocks beneath the ground can be used to heat water, turning it into steam. This steam is then used to drive turbines and generate electricity.

+ **Renewable source of energy**

+ **No pollution and no environmental problems**

− **Very few suitable sites**

− **High cost of drilling** deep into the ground

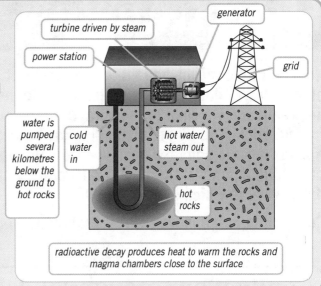

radioactive decay produces heat to warm the rocks and magma chambers close to the surface

Solar energy

The energy carried in the Sun's rays can be converted directly into electricity using solar cells.

Alternatively, the energy carried in the Sun's rays can be absorbed by dark coloured panels and used to heat water.

+ Low maintenance

+ No pollution

+ No need for power cables

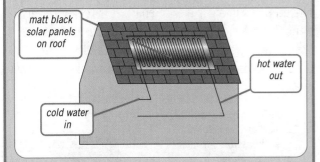

− Initially quite expensive

− May not be so useful in regions where there is limited sunshine

💡 *Make sure you understand the advantages and disadvantages of each of the resources and can justify the choice of a source of energy in a particular situation, e.g. isolated island or mountainous region.*

Biomass

The **chemical energy stored in 'things that have grown'**, e.g. wood, can be **released by burning** them in a power station. This energy source can be maintained by growing a succession of trees and then cropping them when they mature.

+ **Renewable source of energy**

+ **Low level technology** and therefore useful in developing countries

+ Does not add to the greenhouse effect as the carbon dioxide they release when burned was taken from the atmosphere as they grew

− **Large areas of land needed** to grow sufficient numbers of trees

QUICK TEST

❶ Name three ways in which water could be used as an energy resource.

❷ Name two energy resources which may pollute the environment visually.

❸ Name two energy resources which could be easily used and maintained in developing countries.

❹ Name two energy resources which require a suitable site that might be rare.

❺ Name one energy resource that might cause noise pollution.

Heat transfer – conduction

Heat will try to flow when there is a temperature difference between two places. It will flow from the hotter place to the cooler. Sometimes this is desirable and we want to encourage it. Sometimes it is not and we want to try and prevent it. By understanding the different ways in which heat is transferred, we can take measures to improve or reduce its flow rate depending upon the situation. *Conduction*, *convection* and *radiation* are three ways in which heat can move.

Conduction is *the movement of heat by passing on vibration energy*.

Conduction through solids

After five or ten minutes the whole length of this metal rod is hot.

Heat has been transferred along the rod by conduction.

The atoms at the hot end **vibrate more violently as they**

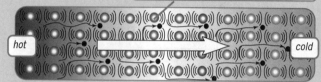

heat carried along metal rod by free electrons and vibrations of atoms

hot — cold

gain energy from the fire. **Free electrons collide with these atoms** and gain energy. The motions of these energetic electrons transfer energy to the cooler end of the rod.

Conductors and insulators 1

All metals are good conductors of heat because:

- their atoms are **packed close together**
- they have **large numbers of free electrons**.

Non-metals are usually poor conductors of heat because:

- their atoms are **further apart**
- there are no **free electrons**.

An **insulator** is a material which **does not allow heat to travel through it easily**. Insulators are used to **prevent or reduce heat transfer**.

Let's have a look at some examples of heat transfer in the home.

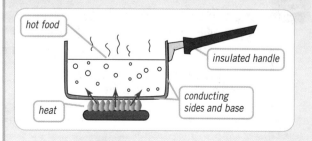

hot food

insulated handle

conducting sides and base

heat

A good saucepan is made from materials that are **conductors** and **insulators**. The base and sides of the pan are made of metal, so that heat is easily conducted from the flame to the food. The handle is made from an insulator, so that it does not become too hot to hold.

The particles in a gas are far apart. It is therefore very difficult for heat to pass through a gas by conduction. Gases are, in fact, excellent insulators and are often used in situations where we want to prevent the flow of heat.

From the above, you should also realise that it is impossible for heat to travel through a vacuum by conduction as it contains no particles.

*Woven materials, e.g. wool and cotton, contain lots of **trapped air** and so are excellent **insulators**. That is why they keep you warm.*

Conductors and insulators 2

Glass fibre is an excellent insulator because it contains large amounts of **trapped air**. It is placed in the loft to **reduce heat loss** through the roof.

It is the layer of air trapped between the two panes of glass that makes double glazing an excellent method of reducing heat loss from a house.

💡 *Try to remember several uses for conductors and insulators, especially around the home.*

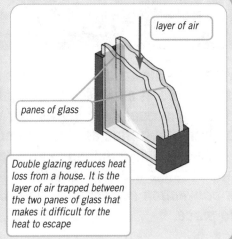

layer of air

panes of glass

Double glazing reduces heat loss from a house. It is the layer of air trapped between the two panes of glass that makes it difficult for the heat to escape

Insulating the home

This diagram shows how heat may escape from a house that has not been insulated.

25% through roof, reduced by putting insulation into loft

10% through windows, reduced by installing double glazing

25% through walls, reduced by having cavity wall insulation

25% through gaps and cracks around doors and windows, reduced by fitting draught excluders

15% through floor, reduced by fitting carpets and underlay

The cost of insulating your home

The table below shows the cost of the different types of insulation that can be used in the home and the annual savings that might result from each.

Type of insulation	Typical cost (£s)	Typical annual saving (£s)	Payback time (years)
double glazing	3000	50	60
cavity wall	500	100	5
loft insulation	250	125	2
draft excluders	100	20	5

💡 *Make sure you understand the idea of cost effectiveness. A question about the cost effectiveness of different types of insulation is asking 'how quickly will the savings pay for the extra insulation'. It is not asking which is the best insulator.*

QUICK TEST

1. What is a conductor?
2. Give one example and one use of a good conductor.
3. What is an insulator?
4. Give one example and one use of an insulator.
5. What is double glazing?
6. Suggest five methods by which you could reduce the heat escaping from your house.

Heat transfer – convection

When the air inside one of these balloons is warmed by its burners, it expands. As a result, it becomes less dense and rises carrying its extra energy with it. If the burners are turned off, the air cools and contracts. It is now more dense and so begins to fall. This movement of air, because of its expansion and contraction, is called a *convection current* and can *transfer energy from place to place*.

Rising warm air will lift these balloons into the sky. But what will happen when the air cools?

Heating a room by convection

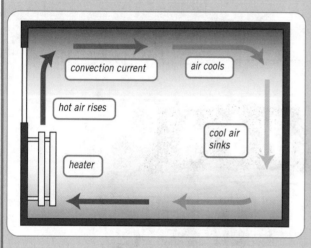

convection current

air cools

hot air rises

cool air sinks

heater

The energy is transferred to all parts of this room by convection.

Note that the warmest air is next to the ceiling. The greatest loss of heat is likely to take place here unless there is insulation above the ceiling.

Traditional open fires are not very efficient at warming a room. They create convection currents that transfer a lot of heat up the chimney, which then escapes to the surroundings.

Convection currents in ovens and fridges

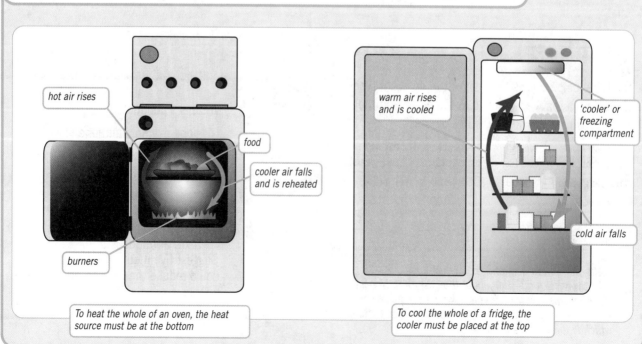

hot air rises

food

cooler air falls and is reheated

burners

warm air rises and is cooled

'cooler' or freezing compartment

cold air falls

To heat the whole of an oven, the heat source must be at the bottom

To cool the whole of a fridge, the cooler must be placed at the top

Convection currents in cavity walls

Many older homes have cavity walls which contain just air. Air is a good insulator and so reduces heat loss by conduction. However, heat can cross the gap if a convection current is set up.

To prevent this from happening, foam insulation can be injected into the cavity. The foam contains lots of trapped air which is unable to move as part of a convection current.

In modern houses, solid foam insulation boards are placed inside the cavity as the house is being built.

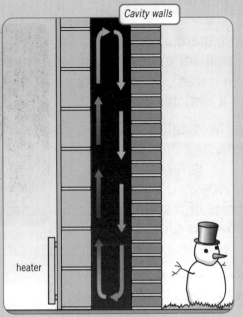

Cavity walls

heater

Injecting foam insulation into the cavity

Solid insulation boards places between the two walls

Sea breezes

It is a common mistake to write that heat rises. It is better to say that, when warmed, a gas becomes less dense and rises, taking heat energy with it.

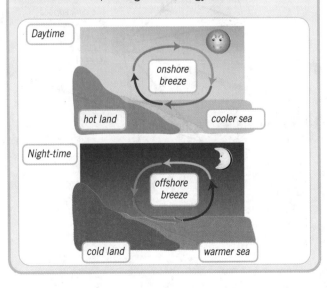

Daytime

onshore breeze

hot land   cooler sea

Night-time

offshore breeze

cold land   warmer sea

QUICK TEST

1. Why does a gas rise when it is warmed?

2. What happens to a gas when it cools?

3. Why are traditional open fires inefficient?

4. Why should foam be placed inside a cavity wall?

5. Where should the freezing compartment of a fridge be placed so it cools the whole of a fridge?

6. In which direction will a sea breeze blow at midday during a hot summer?

Heat transfer – radiation

All bodies *emit* and *absorb* thermal radiation. Thermal radiation is the transfer of heat by *electromagnetic waves* (infrared). The hotter a body is, the more energy it radiates.

The photograph on the right is called a thermogram. It was taken using the radiation emitted by the building. The *different colours indicate different temperatures*. The lighter colours are the hottest parts of the building. The coldest parts are shown as blue.

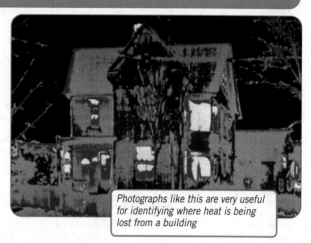

Photographs like this are very useful for identifying where heat is being lost from a building

Heat from the Sun

The transfer of heat by conduction or convection **requires particles**. The transfer of energy by radiation does not. There are no particles between the Sun and the Earth so heat cannot be transferred by conduction or convection. **Heat travels from the Sun to the Earth as waves (radiation).**

Transfer of heat by radiation

Absorption or reflection

When radiation strikes an object it can be either a) **absorbed** or b) **reflected**. Which one occurs depends upon the nature of the surface of the object.

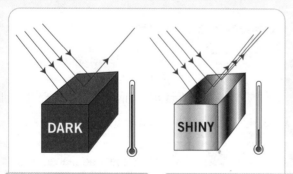

DARK

SHINY

Objects with **dark, rough surfaces** absorb most of the radiation and become warmer

Objects with **light-coloured, shiny surfaces** reflect most of the radiation and will remain cooler

Radiation can be reflected back into a room by placing a sheet of aluminium foil behind the radiator

Solar heater

In hot countries where fuel is scarce, food can be cooked using a solar heater like the one shown below.

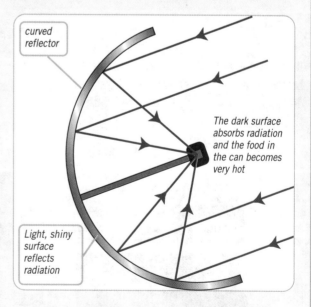

curved reflector

The dark surface absorbs radiation and the food in the can becomes very hot

Light, shiny surface reflects radiation

The light-coloured surface of the curved mirror reflects the heat. The dark matt surface of the can absorbs the heat

Emitting radiation

We can sometimes feel the radiation being given off, or emitted, by an object. How do you know a radiator is hot without touching it?

How much radiation an object emits depends upon a) its **temperature** and b) the nature of its surface.

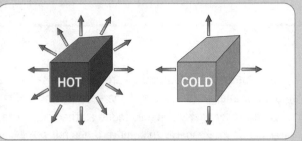

Warm objects give off (emit) heat radiation more than cold objects.

Objects with **dark**, **matt surfaces** give off lots of radiation, i.e. they are **good emitters**.

Objects with **light**, **shiny surfaces** give off less radiation, i.e. they are poor emitters. This can be proved by the simple experiment with teapots – see diagrams on the right.

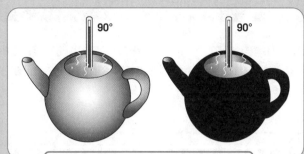

After 20 minutes the water in the black teapot is cooler as it has emitted more radiation

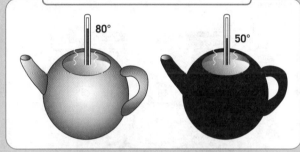

When wrapped in these shiny space blankets athletes will emit less radiation and so will lose body heat more slowly

---

QUICK TEST

1. What kind of radiation is emitted by a hot object?

2. How do we know that heat travels from the Sun to Earth by radiation?

3. What two things might happen when radiation strikes an object?

4. What kind of a surface should an object, which is a good absorber of radiation, have?

5. What kind of a surface should an object, which is a very poor absorber of radiation, have?

6. What is a thermogram?

7. What kind of a surface should an object, which is a good emitter of radiation, have?

8. What kind of a surface should an object, which is a poor emitter of radiation, have?

9. What colour should a radiator be painted so that it can warm a room quickly?

Effects of heat transfer

Absorbing energy may cause an object to become warmer, melt or boil. Losing energy may cause it to become cooler, freeze or condense.

Warming and cooling

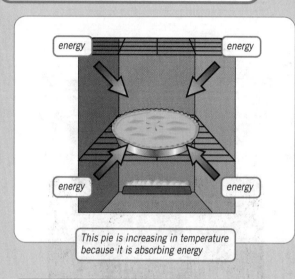

This pie is increasing in temperature because it is absorbing energy

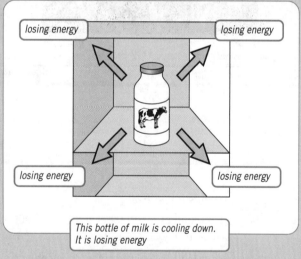

This bottle of milk is cooling down. It is losing energy

How much an object warms up or cools down because of energy transfer depends upon several things:

- the mass of the object
- the amount of energy the object gains or loses
- the material from which the object is made.

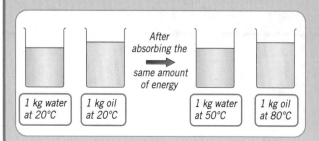

If equal masses of water and oil are given the same amount of energy, the oil would increase its temperature by nearly twice as much as the water. The water needs more energy to achieve the same temperature change.

We describe the different appetites that substances have for energy by using the term **specific heat capacity (c)**. The larger the specific heat capacity of a substance, the more energy it needs to increase its temperature. The specific heat capacity for water is 4200 J/kg/K. This means that 4200 of energy would be needed to increase the temperature of 1 kg of water by 1 K. It also means that 1 kg of water needs to lose 4200 J of energy if its temperature is to decrease by 1 K.

Substance	Specific heat capacity (J/kg/K)
water	4200
copper	380
iron	460
lead	140

The specific heat capacity of a substance is the amount of energy that is necessary to change the temperature of 1 kg of that substance by 1 K.

All the above can be summarised in the equation:

$$E = m \times c \times (T_2 - T_1)$$

where T_1 and T_2 are the initial and final temperatures.

Example 1

Copper has a specific heat capacity of 380 J/kg/K. Calculate the energy that a 3 kg block of copper must gain if its temperature is to increase from 25°C to 75°C.

$$E = 3 \text{ kg} \times 380 \text{ J/kg/K} \times (75 - 25)°C$$
$$= 57\,000 \text{ J or } 57 \text{ kJ}$$

Melting and boiling

Sometimes when an object gains or loses energy, its temperature does not change. Instead, it may change state, i.e. it may melt, freeze, boil or condense.

The energy being given to the water in this kettle is being used to change the state of the water. There is no temperature change

- If water at 100°C is given energy, it will boil and change into steam at the same temperature.
- If energy is taken from steam at 100°C, it will condense and change into water at 100°C.
- If ice at 0°C is given energy, it will melt and change into water at 0°C.
- If energy is taken from water at 0°C, it will freeze and change into ice at 0°C.

The amount of energy that needs to be given to, or taken from, an object in order to change its state, depends upon:

- the mass of the object
- the substance from which the object is made.

We can describe this relationship using the equation:

$$E = m \times L$$

where: E is the energy provided or removed

m is the mass of substance which changes state

L is the specific latent heat of the substance.

The specific latent heat of a substance describes how much energy must be gained or lost to change the state of 1 kg of the substance without changing its temperature.

The specific latent heat of **vaporisation** for water is 2 400 000 J/kg.

The specific latent heat of **fusion** for ice is 340 000 J/kg.

Example 1

Calculate the amount of energy that must be given to 5 kg of water at 100°C in order to change it into steam without changing its temperature.

$$E = m \times L$$
$$= 5 \text{ kg} \times 2\,400\,000 \text{ J/kg}$$
$$= 12\,000\,000 \text{ J or } 12 \text{ MJ}$$

Example 2

Calculate how much energy must be removed from 2 kg of water at 0°C to change it into ice at the same temperature.

$$E = m \times L$$
$$= 2 \text{ kg} \times 340\,000 \text{ J/kg}$$
$$= 680\,000 \text{ J or } 680 \text{ KJ}$$

 Remember, temperature is a measure of how hot an object is and is measured in °C or K. Heat is a form of energy and is measured in J.

QUICK TEST

1 Explain the phrase, 'The specific heat capacity of water is 4.2 kJ/kg/°C'.

2 Calculate the energy released when 2 kg of water cools by 5°C.

3 Calculate the energy needed to increase the temperature of a 5 kg block of iron by 10°C.

4 Explain the phrase, 'The specific latent heat of vaporisation of water is 2.4 MJ'.

5 Calculate the energy needed to boil 10 kg of water without changing its temperature.

6 Explain the phrase 'The specific latent heat of fusion of ice is 340 kJ'.

7 Calculate the energy that must be taken from 3 kg of water at 0°C in order to change it into ice at the same temperature.

Current, charge and resistance

An electric current is *a flow of charge. In metals*, the charges are normally carried *by electrons*. Metals are *good conductors* because they contain lots of electrons that *are able to move around easily*. Non-metals are mainly *poor conductors or insulators*, because *they do not allow charges to move through them easily*.

Making charges flow

The **voltage** of a cell or battery tells us how **much energy** is being given **to each coulomb of charge**. A **1 volt cell** gives **1 joule of energy to each coulomb of charge** that passes through it. A 9 V battery gives 9 J of energy to each coulomb of charge, and so on.

Some batteries have labels which indicate their **capacity** in Amp-hours, e.g. a 40 Amp-hour battery will deliver a current of 1 A for 40 hours or a current of 2 A for 20 hours, etc., before becoming flat.

Measuring current

We **measure current** with an **ammeter**. The size of a current is the **rate at which charge is flowing**.

Charge is measured in coulombs (C).

Current (I) is measured in amps or **amperes (A)**.

1 A is a flow rate of 1 C/s.

Giving energy away

As charges flow around a circuit they **give away the energy** they were given by the cell/battery. This **energy is transferred into other forms** by the components in the circuit. A bulb **transfers** electrical energy into heat and light energy. A resistor **transfers** electrical energy into heat energy. A buzzer **transfers** electrical energy into sound energy. The **voltage or potential difference (p.d.)** tells us **how much energy is transferred** by a component in a circuit. A **p.d. of 1 V** means **1 J of electrical energy is being transferred** into other forms **every time 1 C of charge** passes through a component.

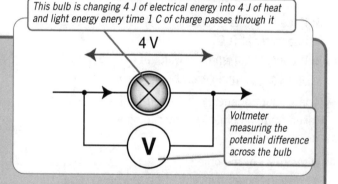

This bulb is changing 4 J of electrical energy into 4 J of heat and light energy enery time 1 C of charge passes through it

4 V

Voltmeter measuring the potential difference across the bulb

We measure the p.d. across a component using **a voltmeter**. This voltmeter is measuring a p.d. of 4 V across the bulb. The bulb is therefore transferring **4 J of electrical energy** into **4 J of heat and light energy** every time **1 C passes through the bulb**.

Electrical resistance

Components in a circuit **resist current** flowing through them.

- If a **small current** flows when a **large p.d.** is applied across a component the component has a **high resistance**.
- If a **large current** flows when a **small p.d.** is applied across a component that component has a **low resistance**.
- We **measure the resistance** of a component in **ohms (Ω)**.
- If a p.d. of 1 V causes a current of 1 A to flow through a component it has a resistance of 1 Ω.

We can write this statement as a formula:

$$R = \frac{V}{I}$$

Example

A current of 3 A flows when a p.d. of 12 V is applied across a wire. Calculate the resistance of the wire.

$$R = \frac{V}{I} = \frac{12\,V}{3\,A} = 4\,\Omega$$

Current-voltage graphs

If a range of p.d.'s are applied across a piece of wire and the currents that flow through it are measured, a **current–voltage graph** can be drawn for the wire. Providing the temperature of the wire does not change, the graph will be a **straight line graph passing through the origin**. This shape of graph shows that the current flowing through the wire is **directly proportional to the** **p.d.** across its ends, providing its temperature does not alter. Some components in a circuit do not produce straight-line current-voltage graphs passing through the origin, e.g. a filament bulb.

As the current flowing through the filament of the bulb increases, its temperature increases, and so too does its resistance.

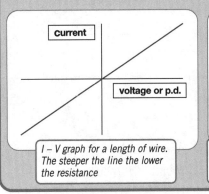

I – V graph for a length of wire. The steeper the line the lower the resistance

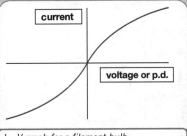

I – V graph for a filament bulb. As the current is increasing, the resistance is increasing, so the graph becomes flatter

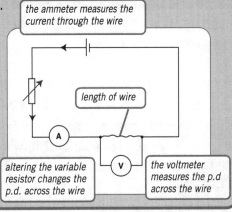

the ammeter measures the current through the wire

length of wire

altering the variable resistor changes the p.d. across the wire

the voltmeter measures the p.d across the wire

Using resistors

We can use **resistors** to **control the size of the current** flowing in a circuit.

If a **variable resistor** is included in a circuit, its value can be altered so that the current flowing in a circuit can be easily changed.

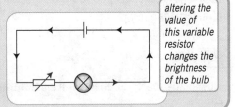

altering the value of this variable resistor changes the brightness of the bulb

Special resistors you need to know about

Light-dependent resistors (LDRs)

These have a **high resistance** when there is **little or no light**. Their resistance **decreases** as **light intensity increases**. They are used in **light-sensitive circuits**, e.g. for controlling **streetlighting or in burglar alarms**.

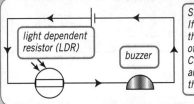

light dependent resistor (LDR)

buzzer

Simple burglar alarm. If the burglar turns on the light the resistance of the LDR falls. Current now flows around the circuit and the buzzer sounds

Thermistors

These are resistors whose **resistance alters greatly as their temperature changes**. Unlike wires, the vast majority of these resistors have **resistances that decrease** as their **temperature increases**.

They are used in **temperature-sensitive circuits**, e.g. **fire alarms and thermostats**.

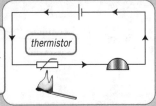

thermistor

Simple fire alarm. If the thermistor becomes warm resistance falls. Current now flows around the circuit and the buzzer sounds.

QUICK TEST

❶ What is an electric current?

❷ What apparatus do we use to measure a) current b) p.d.?

❸ Calculate the resistance of a fixed resistor which has a current of 2 A flowing through it when a p.d. of 9 V is applied across its ends.

❹ What type of resistor decreases its resistance as its temperature increases? Give one use for this type of resistor.

Electrical power

All *electrical appliances* transfer *electrical energy* into *other forms*. A *hairdryer* transfers *electrical energy* into *heat and kinetic* and some *sound energy*. A *radio* transfers *electrical energy* into *sound energy*.

The power of an appliance is a measure of how quickly these energy *changes take place*. This *power rating* is *measured in watts*.

The meaning of power

If a light bulb has a **power rating of 40 W** it transfers **40 J of electrical energy** into heat and light energy **every second**.

If an electrical fire has a **power rating of 2 kW** (2000 W) it **transfers 2000 J of electrical energy** into 2000 J of heat and light energy **every second**.

How many joules of energy have been transferred?

To calculate the total amount of energy an appliance has transferred we use the equation:

Energy = Power x time (in seconds) or E = P x t

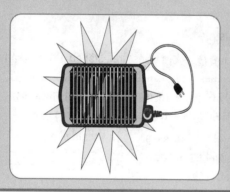

Example

How much electrical energy is converted into heat and light energy when a 60 W bulb is turned on for 5 minutes?

$$E = P \times t = 60 \text{ W} \times 300 \text{ s} = 18\,000 \text{ J or 18 kJ}$$

Draw out the equation E = P x t as a formula triangle. Then try doing some problems where you have to find the values of P or t.

Kilowatt-hours and units

The electricity board measures the energy we use in the home in **kilowatt-hours** or **units**.

They calculate this value using the formula:

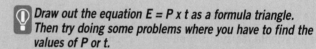

Energy used in kilowatt-hours = power in kilowatts x time in hours

Example

Calculate the energy used when a 3 kW fire is turned on for 2h.

$$E = P \times t = 3 \text{ kW} \times 2 \text{ h} = 6 \text{ kWh or 6 units}$$

The meter and the bill 1

Somewhere in your house is a **meter**, like the one shown on the left. It shows how many units of **electrical energy have been used**. We usually pay our electricity bills every three months, i.e. every quarter. By reading the meter at the beginning and end of the quarter, we can calculate how many units of electrical energy have been used.

The meter and the bill 2

ELECTRICITY BILL				
Charges for electricity used				
Present reading 80139	Previous reading 78579	Units used 1560	Pence per unit 11.00	Charge amount £171.60
Quarterly standing charge Total				£12.00 £183.60

The bill shows the **number of units used** and **the cost per unit**. By multiplying these two values together we can obtain the cost of the electrical energy used. The electricity board will also add to your bill a **standing charge**. This pays for the equipment used by the electricity board in bringing the electricity into your home and its maintenance.

Example

The readings on an electricity meter at the beginning and end of a quarter show that a family has used 800 units. If the cost of one unit is 11p and the standing charge per quarter is £12, calculate the total bill for this household.

$$\text{Cost of electricity} = \text{number of units used} \times \text{cost per unit}$$
$$= 800 \times 11p$$
$$= £88.00$$

If the standing charge is £12, the total cost of the bill is:

$$£88.00 + £12 = £100$$

Calculating the power of an appliance

The power rating of an appliance can be calculated using the formula

Power = Voltage x Current

or

P = V x I

Example

When a voltage of 240 V is applied across a bulb, a current of 0.25 A flows. What is the power rating of this bulb?

$$P = V \times I$$
$$= 240 \times 0.25$$
$$= 60 \text{ W}$$

❶ How many joules of electrical energy are used in the following situations?

a) 100 W bulb turned on for one minute
b) 500 W computer and monitor on for 5 minutes
c) 600 W hairdryer turned on for 2 minutes
d) 1000 W heater turned on for four minutes
e) 2 kW tumble dryer turned on for 5 minutes.

❷ How many kilowatt-hours (units) of electrical energy are converted into other forms in the following situations?

a) 3 kW fire turned on for 3 hours
b) 2 kW tumble dryer used for 30 minutes
c) 1.5 kW water heater turned on for 2 hours
d) 500 W TV turned on for 4 hours
e) 100 W radio turned on for 10 hours.

❸ Calculate the power of an electric fire if a current of 12.5 A flows when it is 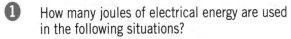 connected to a 240 V supply.

Motors and generators

Motors produce motion using magnetic fields and coils and generators produce currents and voltages, using magnetic fields and coils.

Force on a current-carrying wire

If a **current is passed through a wire** which lies **between the poles of a magnet**, there is a force on the wire. The **force is created by overlapping magnetic fields**.

- In certain places, the fields are in the **same direction**, making the **field here stronger**.
- In certain places the fields are in **opposite directions**, making the **field here weaker**.
- The wire experiences a **force** trying to **push it from the strong part of the field towards the weak part**.

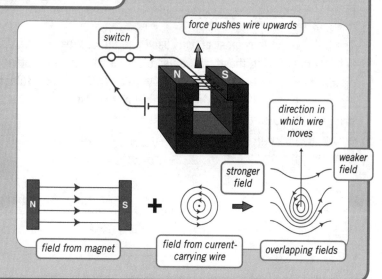

The rotating loop of wire

If the length of wire is replaced by a loop of wire, when current passes around it one side of the loop will feel a force trying to push it upwards. The opposite side of the loop will feel a force trying to push it downwards. The effect of these two forces is to make the **loop rotate**.

This is the basic idea behind the **electric motor**.

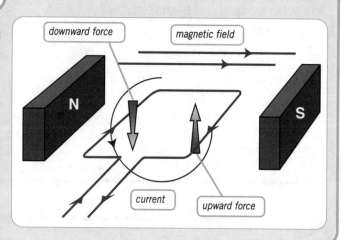

The simple electric motor

For the loop to **rotate continuously**, the direction of the **force** on each side must **change every half turn**, i.e. first a wire must be pushed up then it must be pushed down, etc. This change is achieved using a **split ring commutator**. The split ring **changes the direction of the current** in the coil after **every half turn**.

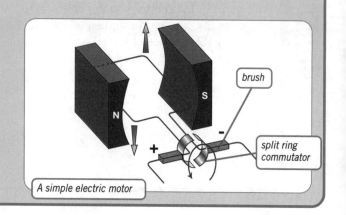

A simple electric motor

Electromagnetic induction

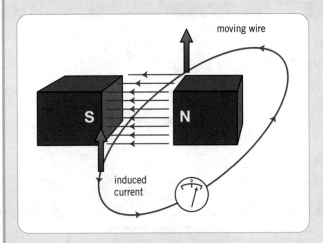

induced current

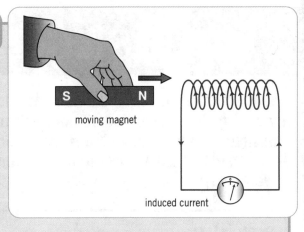

moving magnet

induced current

If a wire is moved (at right angles) across a magnetic field, a voltage is **induced** in the wire. If the wire is **part of a circuit**, a **current will flow**. If the **wire** is moved in the **opposite direction**, the **induced voltage and current** are in the **opposite direction**.

To **increase the size** of the voltage/current we a) use **a stronger magnet** or b) move the wire **more quickly**.

If a magnet **is moved into a coil**, a **voltage/current is induced** in it. If the **magnet is pulled out**, the voltage/current is in **the opposite direction**.

To **increase the size** of the voltage/current, we can a) use a **stronger magnet** b) **move the magnet faster** c) put **more turns on the coil**.

In both experiments, the voltages/currents are being created by a process called **electromagnetic induction**. It is this process which is the basis of all generators and alternators.

Generators and alternators

If a coil is **rotated** between the poles of a magnet, a **current is induced** in the coil. Because the wires are continually **changing direction** as they rotate, the **induced current** also **changes size and direction**. The induced current is an **alternating current**. A **generator** which produces **alternating current** is called an **alternator**.

The coil will generate a larger current if a) a **stronger magnet** is used, b) the coil is **turned more quickly** or c) a coil with **more turns** is used.

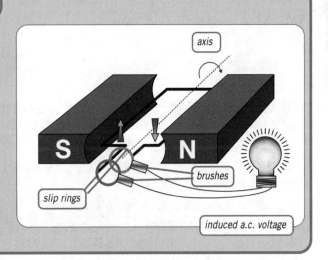

axis

brushes

slip rings

induced a.c. voltage

1. What device changes the direction of the current in an electric motor every half turn?

2. State three ways of increasing the rate of rotation of an electric motor.

3. Why are several coils used in practical motors rather than just one?

4. What kind of current is produced by an alternator?

5. Suggest two ways in which an alternator can be changed to produce a higher current.

Domestic electricity

The electricity we use in the home is known as *mains electricity*. It is generated at a power station and then transmitted to us through the *National Grid*. It is different from the electricity we use from cells and batteries in several ways.

a.c./d.c.

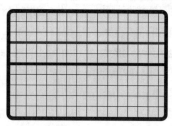

an instrument called the Cathode Ray Oscilloscope shows the type of current and voltage

The horizontal line shows current/voltage has a steady value and passes in one direction. This is d.c. current from a cell or battery

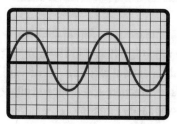

The electricity we get from the mains is a.c. (alternating current)

The 'wave-shaped' line shows an a.c. current voltage which is continually changing direction

The electricity we get from cells and batteries is **one-way electricity**. It is called **direct current (d.c.)**. The electricity from the mains is **continuously changing** direction. It is **alternating current (a.c.). It flows back and forth 50 times every second**, i.e. it has a **frequency of 50 Hz.**

The 3-pin plug

The voltage of the electricity from cells and batteries is quite low, e.g. 9 V, 12 V. **The voltage from the mains is about 230 V**. It **can be dangerous if not used safely. Most appliances** are therefore **connected** to the mains using **insulated plugs.**

It is very important that the wires in a plug are connected to **the correct pins**. Looking at an open plug like the one shown on the right, the **BR**own wire goes to the **B**ottom **R**ight and the **BL**ue wire goes to the **B**ottom **L**eft. The green-and-yellow wire (earth) goes to the top pin.

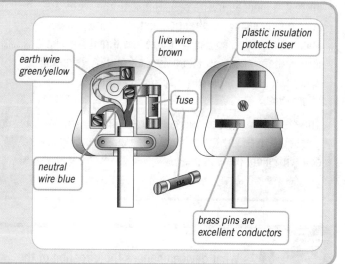

earth wire green/yellow

live wire brown

plastic insulation protects user

fuse

neutral wire blue

brass pins are excellent conductors

Fuses 1

All 3-pin UK plugs contain a **fuse**. This usually consists of a small **cylinder or cartridge** containing a thin piece of **wire with a low melting point.**

If a fault develops in a circuit and **too much current passes** through the fuse, the **wire melts**. The circuit becomes **incomplete** and **current ceases to pass through it.**

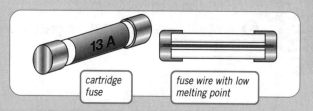

13 A

cartridge fuse

fuse wire with low melting point

The fuse **protects the user** and **limits any damage** to the electrical appliance.

Fuses 2

Fuses are given a **rating** which indicates the **maximum current** that can flow through it without it melting. The most common fuses in the UK have ratings of **1 A, 3 A, and 13 A**.

Which fuse?

Choosing the correct value of fuse for a circuit is important. If the fuse selected has too low a rating, it will melt (blow) and turn off the circuit even when there is no fault and the correct current is flowing. If the fuse has too high a rating, it will not protect the circuit when too large a current flows. The correct value of a fuse is one which is **just large enough to allow the correct current to flow**, e.g. if the normal current is 2 A then a 3 A fuse is selected.

Calculating the correct value

If we know the **power rating of an appliance** connected to the mains supply we can calculate the correct fuse that should be used in this circuit using the equation:

$$I = \frac{P}{V}$$

Example

Calculate the correct fuse needed for a fire rated at 240 V 3 kW.

$$I = \frac{P}{V} = \frac{3000}{240} = 12.5 \text{ A}$$

The correct fuse to use would therefore be a 13 A fuse.

Circuit breakers

These are a **special kind of fuse** which cause a break in a circuit if too much current flows. Once the fault has been put right, the fuse is **usually reset by pushing a button**.

Residual circuit breakers like the one shown below are often used when mowing the lawn or using hedge trimmers. They will detect current flowing to earth if a cable is cut. The instant this happens, the supply is turned off so that the user comes to no harm.

A residual circuit breaker

The earth wire

A 3-pin plug usually has three wires connected to it.

- The **electrical energy** travels into an appliance through the **live wire**.
- The **neutral wire** is the **return path** for the current.
- The earth wire is a safety connection which **protects the user** if an appliance becomes faulty.

If the kettle has a metal casing and the heating element is broken, anyone touching the casing will receive an **electric shock**. With the **earth wire connected**, the user is safe and will not receive an electric shock. This **current blows the fuse that is protecting the user**. Modern appliances, such as kettles, now have **plastic casings** to further reduce the risk of an electric shock for the user. The kettle in this diagram has **double insulation**.

QUICK TEST

1. What kind of current is supplied through the mains?

2. In a typical domestic plug, what colour is
   a) the live wire,
   b) the earth wire and
   c) the neutral wire?

3. Why are the pins of the domestic plug made from copper or brass?

4. Name one advantage of a circuit breaker over a cylinder fuse.

5. Give two situations when a residual circuit breaker might be used.

Waves

Types of wave

Waves transfer energy by vibrations. There are two main types of waves. These are **transverse waves** and **longitudinal waves**.

A **transverse wave** has vibrations across or at right angles to the direction in which the wave is moving. Examples of transverse waves include light waves and surface water waves.

A **longitudinal wave** has vibrations that are along the direction in which the wave is moving. Sound waves are longitudinal waves.

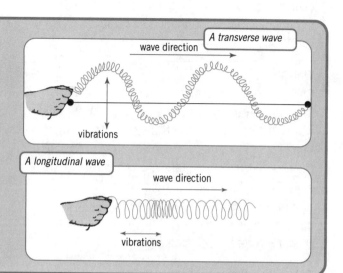

A transverse wave
wave direction
vibrations

A longitudinal wave
wave direction
vibrations

The important bits

The **amplitude** of a wave is the height of a crest or depth of a trough from the undisturbed position.

The **wavelength** of a wave is the distance between successive crests.

The **frequency** of a wave is the number of complete waves

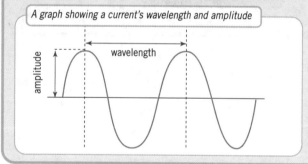

A graph showing a current's wavelength and amplitude

amplitude | wavelength

produced each second by the source. It is measured in hertz (**Hz**). A wave has a frequency of 200 Hz if the source is producing 200 waves each second. We can also describe the frequency of a wave as being the number of waves which passes a point each second.

The velocity of a wave (v), its frequency (f) and its wavelength (λ) are related by the equation:

$$v = f \times \lambda$$

Example

A sound wave has a frequency of 170 Hz and a wavelength of 2 m. Calculate the velocity of this wave.

$$v = f \times \lambda = 170 \times 2 = 340 \text{ m/s}$$

Key properties of waves

When a wave strikes a plane surface it is **reflected** so that the angle of incidence is equal to the angle of reflection. When a wave travels across the boundary between two different mediums its speed and direction may change, i.e. the wave is **refracted**. If the wave slows, it is refracted towards the normal. If the wave speeds up, it is refracted away from the normal.

If a wave is travelling from a more dense medium into a less dense medium and it strikes the boundary at an angle greater than the critical angle, the wave will be **totally internally reflected**.

If a wave travels through a gap or across the edge of an object it may spread out. This process is called **diffraction** and is most noticeable if the size of the gap is the same as the wavelength of the wave.

Seismic waves

Seismic waves are **shock waves** caused by **earthquakes**. They travel through the Earth, starting from the **epicentre**. Seismic waves can cause tremendous damage to buildings and structures on the Earth's surface. There are two types of seismic waves. They are called **P-waves** and **S-waves**.

P-waves and S-waves

P-waves:
- are **longitudinal waves** that can travel through **solids and liquids**
- cause the surface of the Earth and buildings to vibrate **up and down**
- travel slightly **faster than S-waves**
- travel **faster the more dense** the material through which they are travelling.

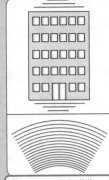

P-waves push buildings up and down

S-waves:
- are **transverse waves** that can only **travel through solids and not through liquids**
- cause **side-to-side vibrations** on the surface
- travel slightly **slower than P-waves**
- travel **faster the more dense** the material through which they are travelling.

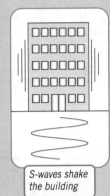

S-waves shake the building

Summary

The Earth is not a solid ball of rock, it has a layered structure.

- The crust is a thin outer layer.
- The mantle is a hot solid which has some liquid properties, i.e. it can flow but extremely slowly, like really thick tar.
- The outer core is a very hot liquid made of molten iron and nickel.
- The inner core is a very hot solid.

💡 *Make sure you can link the properties of the S-waves and P-waves with the structure of the Earth. See Key thoughts and Observations and conclusions.*

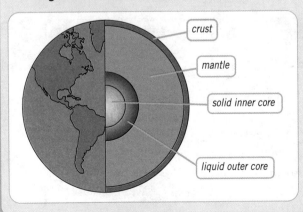

crust

mantle

solid inner core

liquid outer core

Making good use of seismic waves

Knowing the properties of P-waves and S-waves allows scientists to use them to learn about the **internal structure of the Earth**. The paths taken by seismic waves as they travel through the Earth can be monitored using **seismographs**.

Key thoughts
- If the density of the rocks changes, the speeds of the S-waves and P-waves change.
- If their **speeds change**, their **direction usually changes too**.
- If the **change in rock density is gradual**, the paths followed by the waves are **gently curved**.
- If the **change in density is abrupt**, e.g. crossing a boundary between different types of rock, there will be an **abrupt change in direction**.
- If there are **no S-waves**, it suggests there is **liquid rock**.

Observations and conclusions

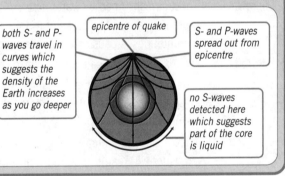

both S- and P-waves travel in curves which suggests the density of the Earth increases as you go deeper

epicentre of quake

S- and P-waves spread out from epicentre

no S-waves detected here which suggests part of the core is liquid

QUICK TEST

1. What do waves carry from place to place?
2. Explain the phrase 'a wave has a frequency of 25 Hz'.
3. Give one example of a) a transverse wave and b) a longitudinal wave.
4. A water wave has a frequency of 5 Hz and a wavelength of 3 m. Calculate the velocity of this wave.
5. What are the names of the two different types of waves produced by an earthquake?
6. Name three differences between these waves.
7. Why do we think that part of the core is liquid?

The electromagnetic spectrum

This is a *family of waves* with a *large number of common properties*. They all:

- can *travel through a vacuum*
- *travel at the same speed* through a vacuum, i.e. the speed of light
- are *transverse waves*
- transfer energy
- can be *reflected*, *absorbed*, *transmitted*, *refracted* and *diffracted*.

Some of the *properties* of these waves *change* as their *wavelength and frequency* changes. The family is therefore divided into seven smaller groups.

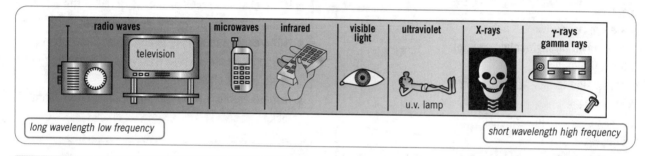

Biological effects of exposure to electromagnetic waves

Radio waves	No known effect.
Microwaves	These are absorbed by water molecules causing body tissue to warm. Large doses can cause burns. The rapid increase in the usage of mobile phones and the erection of microwave transmitter masts close to communities is causing concern over the possible long-term effects of exposure to microwaves.
Infrared	Overexposure can cause burning to the skin.
Visible light	This causes the chemical changes on the retina of the eye, which makes vision possible. Overexposure, e.g. looking directly at the Sun, can cause damage to the retina resulting in impaired vision or blindness.
Ultraviolet	These cause chemical changes in the skin resulting in tanning and premature aging. Excessive exposure will result in sunburn and possibly skin cancer. Sun blocks prevent the radiation from reaching the skin.
X-rays	These are highly penetrating rays which can cause cancer and kill living cells. Workers exposed to X-rays, e.g. radiographers, wear lead aprons or stand behind lead screens as X-rays cannot penetrate lead.
Gamma rays	Emitted by some radioactive materials, they are also very penetrating and can cause cancer and kill living cells.

Radio waves

Radio waves are used for **communicating over large distances**. Short wavelength radio waves are used for television broadcasting and FM radio. Longer wavelength radio waves are used for traditional AM radio.

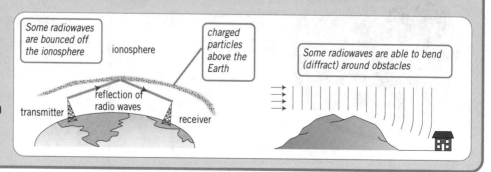

Microwaves

Some microwaves pass easily through the Earth's atmosphere and so are used for **communications via satellites**, e.g. **mobile phones**. Some microwaves are used for **cooking**, e.g. **microwave ovens**. Water molecules inside food absorb microwaves.
They become 'hot', cooking the food from the inside.

Microwaves can be dangerous if misused. They **can cause damage to living cells**.

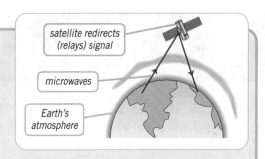

satellite redirects (relays) signal

microwaves

Earth's atmosphere

Infrared waves (heat radiation)

Infrared waves are **given out by all warm objects**. Our skin can sense or detect the infrared waves. Overexposure causes **sunburn** but not tanning.

Infrared waves are used to **'see in the dark'**. Special **'heat-seeking'** cameras **create images** of objects using the **infrared waves they are emitting**. These are often used by the emergency services to detect people trapped in collapsed buildings or lost in mountains or on moors.

Remote controls for TVs, radios, etc. use infrared waves to carry instructions.

Visible light

We use these waves to **see**. It is the one part of the electromagnetic spectrum to which our **eyes are sensitive**.

Visible light is used to carry messages down **optical fibres**.

We use visible light to see

Ultraviolet

Ultraviolet waves are **emitted by the Sun**. They **cause our skins to tan**. Overexposure to ultraviolet waves **can lead to skin cancer**.

When certain chemicals are exposed to ultraviolet they **fluoresce (glow)**. Words written with security markers are only visible in ultraviolet light. Ultraviolet light can be used to detect forged banks notes by fluorescence.

X-rays

X-rays have a very **short wavelength** and a very **high frequency**. They are **highly penetrating**. X-rays are used to look for damaged bones inside the body. Overexposure can cause cancer. Radiographers therefore **stand behind lead screens** or **wear lead aprons** to **prevent over exposure**.

X-rays were used to monitor the development of foetus in the womb during pregnancy but ultrasound is used now, as it is less likely to cause any damage to the unborn baby.

Gamma rays

These are very **penetrating waves** which are **emitted by some radioactive materials**. They can be used to kill harmful bacteria, e.g. sterilise surgical equipment. If used correctly, they can be used to kill certain kinds of cancer (this is known as radiotherapy).

Incorrect exposure/dosage can **damage living cells and cause cancer**.

QUICK TEST

❶ Name two properties all these waves have in common.

❷ Name three groups of waves that can be used for communications.

❸ Name three groups of waves that might cause cancer.

❹ Name two types of waves that we as human beings can sense.

Analogue and digital signals

Analogue signals which travel along copper wires are being replaced by digital signals which travel along optical fibres.

Total internal reflection and optical fibres

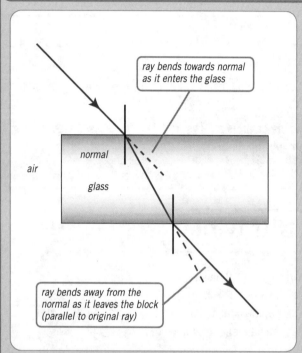

ray bends towards normal as it enters the glass

air

normal

glass

ray bends away from the normal as it leaves the block (parallel to original ray)

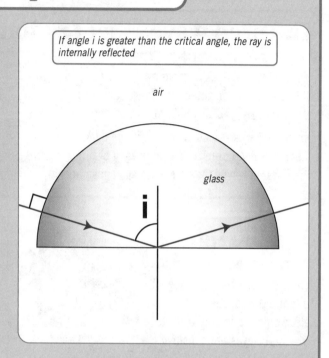

If angle *i* is greater than the critical angle, the ray is internally reflected

air

glass

i

When a ray of light enters a glass block at an angle, it **slows down** and bends towards **the normal**. This change in direction is called **refraction**. When the ray emerges from the block it **speeds up** and bends **away from the normal**.

If a ray leaving a glass block strikes the boundary at an angle **greater than the critical angle** then **total internal reflection** takes place, i.e. the ray is not refracted but reflected.

In modern telecommunications systems, **optical fibres** are being used to replace traditional **copper wires** to carry signals. The light signals in optical fibres undergo total internal reflection.

An optical fibre has a **high-density glass for its core** and a **less dense glass as an outer coating**. The fibre is so narrow that light entering at one end will always strike the boundary between the two glasses at an angle greater than the critical angle. It will therefore undergo a **series of total internal reflections** before emerging at the far end.

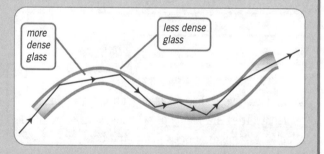

more dense glass

less dense glass

The advantages of using optical fibres
- The fibres are cheaper than copper wires
- They are lighter
- They can carry more signals
- The signals they carry are more secure.

Communicating using analogue signals

As radio waves and microwaves travel from an emitter towards a receiver, there may be some **loss in signal strength**, possibly due to **diffraction or interference**. To ensure a strong signal arrives at the receiver, it may be **amplified** several times at **repeater stations**.

Analogue signals vary continuously. When they are amplified at relay stations any **distortions (noise)** which have been added to the wave during its journey will also be **amplified**. If the noise is considerable, the final signal received may be very different from the original and therefore difficult to understand.

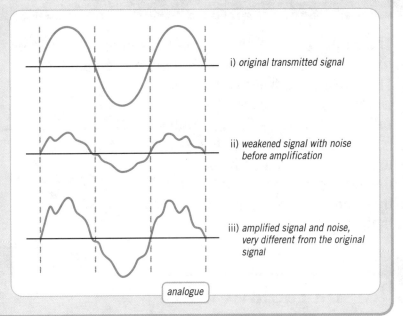

i) *original transmitted signal*

ii) *weakened signal with noise before amplification*

iii) *amplified signal and noise, very different from the original signal*

analogue

Communicating using digital signals

Digital signals have only two values: 1 and 0. An analogue signal can be converted into a digital signal, i.e. its continuously changing shape can be described by a code **consisting of just 1s and 0s**. This code can then be transmitted. When the weakened signal arrives at a repeater station, it is easy to recognise, even with lots of noise, those parts of the signal which should be a 1 and those that should be a 0. These are amplified, producing a **perfect copy of the original**. At the receiver, the digital code is converted back into the analogue signal, but without any noise distortion, i.e. the signal is very clear.

> The key things to remember here are the advantages in using digital signals rather than analogue.

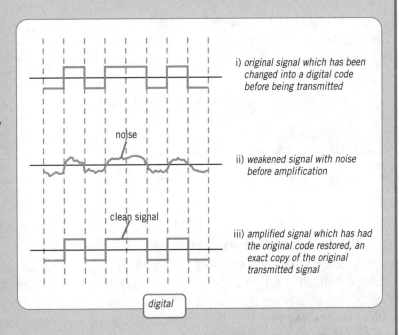

i) *original signal which has been changed into a digital code before being transmitted*

noise

ii) *weakened signal with noise before amplification*

clean signal

iii) *amplified signal which has had the original code restored, an exact copy of the original transmitted signal*

digital

QUICK TEST

1. Why is light unable to escape through the sides of an optical fibre?

2. Give three reasons why optical fibres are replacing copper wires in telecommunications networks.

3. Why do signals need to pass through a repeater station?

4. What is noise?

5. How does noise affect an analogue signal?

6. What happens to the noise on an analogue signal when it passes through a repeater station?

7. What effect does this have on the final signal received?

8. What is the main advantage of using digital signals rather than analogue?

Nuclear radiation

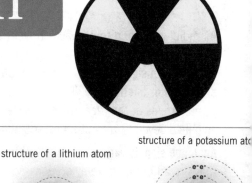

The nuclei of some atoms give out *radiation* all of the time. These substances are said to be *radioactive*. There are three types of radiation which might be emitted: *alpha*, *beta* and *gamma* radiation. These nuclear radiations can be very useful. They can also be very dangerous. It is important, therefore, that we understand their properties.

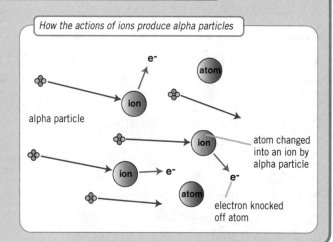

It is the nuclei of atoms that emit different types of radiation

structure of a helium atom

structure of a lithium atom

structure of a potassium ato

An atom has a central core called a nucleus which contains two types of particles called protons and neutrons. Very small particles called electrons orbit the nucleus

Alpha radiation (α)

Alpha particles are **slow-moving helium nuclei**, i.e. they consist of **two protons and two neutrons**. They are **big and heavy** and so have **poor penetration** (just a few centimetres in air). They collide with lots of atoms, **knocking some of their electrons off** and **creating ions**. They are **very good ionisers**.

An **ion** is an atom that has become charged by either losing or gaining electrons. They are **positively charged** and so can be **deflected by electric and magnetic fields**.

How the actions of ions produce alpha particles

alpha particle

atom changed into an ion by alpha particle

electron knocked off atom

Beta radiation (β)

These are **fast moving electrons**. They are small and therefore have **quite good penetrating powers** (up to about a metre in air). They do collide with atoms and produce ions but not as many as the alpha particles. They are **negatively charged** and so can be **deflected by electric and magnetic fields**.

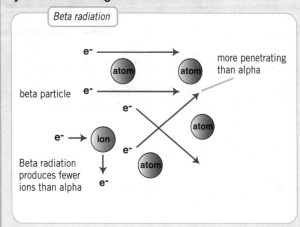

Beta radiation

beta particle

more penetrating than alpha

Beta radiation produces fewer ions than alpha

Gamma rays (γ)

These are **short wavelength, electromagnetic waves**, similar to X-rays. They **travel at the speed of light** and are **very penetrating** (and can travel almost unlimited distances through air). They don't hit many atoms as they travel through a material and so are **very poor ionisers**. Gamma radiation **carries no charge** and so is **unaffected by magnetic and electric fields**.

> *It is very important in this topic to remember the different properties of the different types of radiation.*

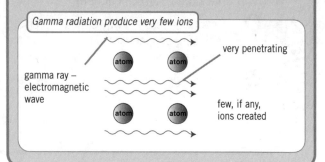

Gamma radiation produce very few ions

gamma ray – electromagnetic wave

very penetrating

few, if any, ions created

Comparison of the properties of alpha, beta and gamma radiation

Radiation	α	β	γ
Mass	4	negligible (1/2000)	0
Charge	+2	–1	0
Relative ionising power	100 000	1000	1
Approximate penetrating power in air	1–5 cm	10-80 cm	almost unlimited

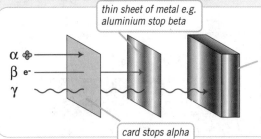

α ⊕
β e⁻
γ

thin sheet of metal e.g. aluminium stop beta

card stops alpha

thick sheet of dense metal or several metres of concrete is needed to stop gamma

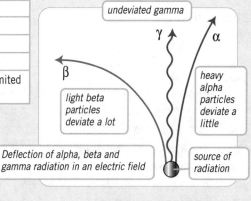

undeviated gamma

γ   α

β

light beta particles deviate a lot

heavy alpha particles deviate a little

Deflection of alpha, beta and gamma radiation in an electric field

source of radiation

Background radiation

There are radioactive substances all around us. Some of them are manmade and used in hospitals, nuclear power stations and even in the home. Most of the radioactive substances around us are naturally occurring. They are in the ground, in the food we eat, they are even in the air we breathe. Some radiation reaches us from space.

The radiation produced by these sources is called **background radiation**.

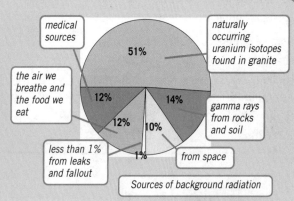

medical sources

naturally occurring uranium isotopes found in granite

51%

the air we breathe and the food we eat

12%

14%

gamma rays from rocks and soil

12%

10%

less than 1% from leaks and fallout

1%

from space

Sources of background radiation

Exposure to radiation

Absorption of any of the three types of radiation by living cells is potentially dangerous.

Absorption may cause **cell damage** and lead to illnesses such as **cancer**. Higher levels of exposure to these radiations may **kill living cells**. Those at most risk, e.g. radiographers, wear **radiation badges**. These contain photographic film which, when developed, show the **degree of exposure** to radiation for that worker.

Other ways in which to reduce exposure to radiation are by:

- wearing protective clothing
- handling radioactive materials at a distance, e.g. using tongs
- limiting exposure time.

Exposure from sources outside the body

- Alpha radiation is the least dangerous as it is the least penetrating and unlikely to pass through the skin.
- Beta and gamma radiations are more dangerous because they are more penetrating.

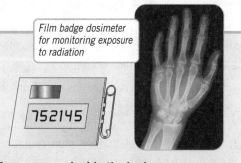

Film badge dosimeter for monitoring exposure to radiation

752145

Exposure from sources inside the body

- Alpha is the most dangerous radiation as it is most strongly absorbed by living cells and therefore causes most damage.
- Beta and gamma rays are not so dangerous as they are less likely to be absorbed by living cells.

QUICK TEST

 Which type of radiation:

a) is most penetrating?
b) is the best ioniser?
c) is negatively charged?
d) is a fast moving electron?
e) is an electromagnetic wave?

Uses of radioactivity

Radioactive materials are used in industry, in hospitals and even in our homes.

Choosing the right source

The amount and type of radiation emitted each second by a source (**the activity**) depends upon the number and type of **unstable nuclei** present. As time goes by, the number of unstable nuclei in a sample decreases. How quickly they decrease is described using the idea of a **half-life**. A half-life describes how long it will take for half of the unstable nuclei in a sample to **decay**. Some nuclei have very short half-lives and some very long. This is just one of the factors to be considered when choosing which radioactive material to use for a particular job.

Some examples of half-lives

Uranium 238	4500 million years
Radium 226	1620 years
Strontium 90	28 days
Radon 222	4 days
Radium 214	20 minutes

○ undecayed atom   ● decayed atom

large number of unstable nuclei – lots of radiation emitted

fewer unstable nuclei – less radiation emitted

1   *half-life*   2

3   *half-life*   4

after each half-life the number of undecayed nuclei halves

after each half-life the activity of the source halves

Quality control

Sheet material, such as paper, needs to be produced with a constant thickness. This can be monitored using the emissions from a radioactive source.

- A beta-emitting source, such as strontium-90, is placed above the paper.
- A beta detector is placed directly beneath it.
- If the paper becomes thinner, more radiation reaches the detector and the pressure between the rollers is decreased.

paper   rollers   source of beta radiation

machine to adjust pressure on rollers   detector   sheet of constant thickness

- If the paper becomes thicker, less radiation is detected and the pressure on the rollers is increased.
- Continuous monitoring like this guarantees that the thickness/quality of the paper is correct.
- This arrangement can also be used to monitor the quality of sheet metal but a gamma-emitting source replaces the stontium-90.

Radioactive tracers

Radioisotopes can be used to monitor the flow of liquids and gases in pipes. A gamma-emitting radioisotope is added to the fluid flowing through the pipe. This material is called a tracer. If there is a leak in the pipe, a higher concentration of gamma radiation will be detected.

Using a radioisotope in this manner avoids the need to dig up whole sections of roads and piping in order to find the leak. Tracers can also be used to check the progress of fluids, such as blood and digested food, through the body. For example, sodium-24 is a radioisotope that can be introduced into the body to check for internal bleeding.

fluid 'labelled' with gamma emitter

radiation is high where the pipe is leaking

Radiotherapy

Some forms of cancer can be removed by surgery. Others, like brain tumours, because of their position, may require a different solution, e.g. radiotherapy.

- A narrow beam of radiation is directed at the tumour from different positions.
- A high dose of radiation, which is needed to kill the cancerous cells, only occurs within the tumour.
- In other places, the dose is not large enough to cause cell damage.

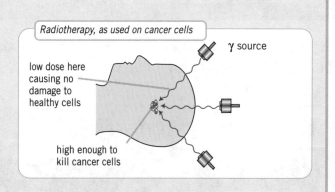

Radiotherapy, as used on cancer cells

γ source

low dose here causing no damage to healthy cells

high enough to kill cancer cells

Sterilisation

Food rots because of the presence and growth of bacteria. Cooling and freezing slows down the growth of the bacteria but does not prevent it. If food is exposed to gamma radiation before being frozen, the bacteria are killed and the food keeps for much longer. This process is called sterilisation.

Surgical instruments used to be sterilised by putting them in boiling water. Nowadays these instruments are sterilised by exposing them to gamma radiation.

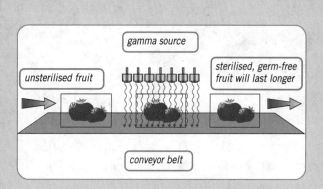

gamma source

unsterilised fruit

sterilised, germ-free fruit will last longer

conveyor belt

Smoke detectors

Some smoke detectors, like the one shown below, contain a small amount of americium-241. This is an alpha emitter. The emitted alpha particles collide with air molecules within the smoke detector creating ions. This in turn creates a very small current. If smoke enters the detector, this current stops or decreases. It is this change in current which triggers the alarm.

One big advantage of this type of smoke detector is that, when the battery is towards the end of its life, this too causes the current to fall and the alarm sounds indicating that the battery needs replacing.

> *This is a very popular topic in exams. Make sure you can explain some of these uses.*

QUICK TEST

1. What kind of radiation should a source emit if it is to be used for monitoring the thickness of a) card and b) sheets of steel?

2. What is the name given to a radioisotope which is injected into a fluid so that its flow can be monitored?

3. Why should a source which emits alpha radiation not be used to check the flow of blood through a body?

4. What is the treatment of cancer with radiation called?

5. Which type of radiation is used to sterilise surgical instruments?

6. What causes a current to flow in a smoke detector?

The Earth in space

We live on a *planet* called *Earth*. It is one of many bodies that together form our solar system.

The solar system

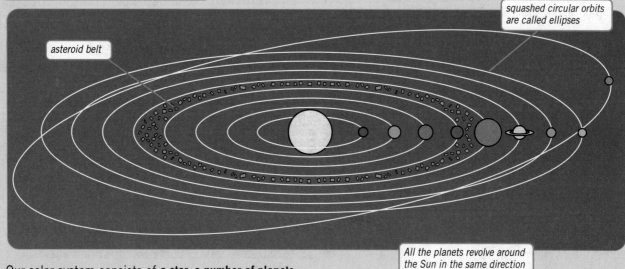

squashed circular orbits are called ellipses

asteroid belt

All the planets revolve around the Sun in the same direction

Our solar system consists of **a star, a number of planets, moons, asteroids and comets**. We call our **star the Sun**. It contains over 99% of all the mass in our solar system. The planets, their moons, the asteroids and the comets all orbit the Sun.

The Earth is one of nine planets. In order, starting with the planet nearest the Sun, they are Mercury, Venus, Earth, Mars, Jupiter, Saturn, Uranus, Neptune and Pluto. We can remember the order using the sentence: **M**any **V**ery **E**nergetic **M**en **J**og **S**lowly **U**pto **N**ewport **P**agnell.

We see stars like the Sun because of the light they emit. **Stars are luminous** objects.

We see **planets and moons** because of the light they reflect. They are **non-luminous** objects.

Comets

Comets are **large rock-like pieces of ice** that orbit the Sun. They have very elliptical orbits. Comets **travel fastest** when they are **close to the Sun** because the **gravitational forces here are large**.

When close to the Sun, some of a **comet's ice melts creating a long tail**. Their velocities are lowest when they are a long way from the Sun.

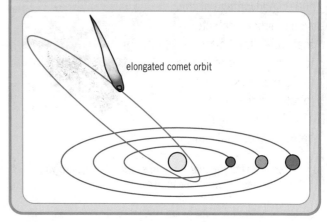

elongated comet orbit

Gravitational forces

The planets move in orbits because they are being **'pulled' by the gravity of the Sun**. This force is called a centripetal force. Objects which are **closest to the Sun feel the strongest pull** and follow the **most curved paths**.

Objects that are a **long way from the Sun feel the weakest pull** and follow the **least curved orbits**.

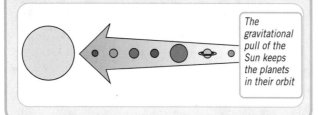

The gravitational pull of the Sun keeps the planets in their orbit

Meteors and meteorites

Meteors are small fragments of rocks and dust which enter the Earth's atmosphere. As they fall they become very hot and are seen as streaks of light.

Very rarely some meteors reach the surface of the Earth. These space rocks are now called **meteorites**. It is thought that most meteors are dust and debris left behind by passing comets.

Satellites

Moons are **large natural satellites** that **orbit a planet**.

We have just one moon but some planets have several, e.g. Mars has two, Jupiter has 16 and Saturn has 21.

Artificial satellites

Artificial satellites launched by man can be put into orbit around the Earth. They have three main uses:

1 To look away from Earth into deep space, e.g. the Hubble telescope.

2 To monitor conditions on the surface of the Earth e.g. weather satellites. Satellites that monitor the Earth's surface are often put into low polar orbits.

3 To stay above the same place on the Earth's surface the whole time, e.g. communications satellites. These are called **geostationary satellites**.

Skylab

Asteroids

Asteroids are lumps of rock orbiting the Sun. They vary in size from several metres to about 1000 km in diameter. **Most asteroids** are found **in a belt** between **Mars and Jupiter**. Some scientists believe that this asteroid belt is the remains of a planet which was destroyed, perhaps by the large gravitational field of Jupiter. Others think that, perhaps in the past, a planet failed to form here and the asteroids are the remains of the material from which the planet might have been made.

There are some asteroids which are found travelling outside the asteroid belt. If a large asteroid collided with the Earth it could wipe out life as we know it. Is this likely to happen? The answer is yes. It has happened in the past creating large craters in the Earth's surface. There is no reason to believe that it will not happen in the future, but no one knows when. Hopefully before it happens we will have developed the technology to prevent the collision or evacuate the Earth. Already some scientists are suggesting that we set up a programme to look out into space and search for Near Earth Objects (NEOs) which might threaten the Earth.

There are many craters on the surface of the Moon caused by meteors and asteroids.

QUICK TEST

1 Name one body in the sky which is a) luminous and b) non-luminous.

2 What forces keep all the planets in orbit around the Sun?

3 Where during their orbit of the Sun do comets travel fastest?

4 What is an NEO and why is it a threat to the Earth?

5 What is a natural satellite?

6 Give three uses for artificial satellites.

Stars and the universe

Our Sun is a *star*. It is just one of billions of stars that make up the *galaxy* we live in.

Our galaxy is called the *Milky Way*. There are billions of galaxies in the *universe*. They are separated by distances that are often millions of times greater than the distances between stars within a galaxy

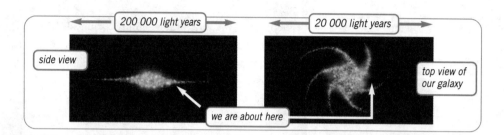

200 000 light years

20 000 light years

side view

top view of our galaxy

we are about here

How stars are born

Stars form when **particles of dust and gas** are pulled together by **gravitational forces**. These forces **compress** the particles together so tightly that there is a **very large increase in temperature**. This temperature increase sets off **nuclear reactions** which **fuse hydrogen atoms** together. These reactions release large amounts of energy as heat and light. **Smaller concentrations of gases** may form some distance away from the developing star. These may eventually **become planets and their moons**.

The life of a star 1

Stars change gradually with time. When a star first forms, **gravitational forces pull matter together**. When the **nuclear reactions begin**, the high temperatures create forces which try to make the **gases expand**. When these **two forces are balanced**, the star is said to be in its **main stable period**. This period may last for millions of years. Our Sun is in this stable period.

Towards the end of the stable period, new hydrogen nuclei are becoming scarce and new nuclear reactions between helium nuclei occur. As a result, the **star begins to expand** and becomes a little **cooler**. The star is changing into a **red giant**.

Some time later, the helium nuclei become scarce and new nuclear reactions begin, but on this occasion, the expansive forces are less than the **forces of gravity** causing the star to **contract**. The star is now changing into a white dwarf. The matter from which **white dwarf** stars is made is millions of times more dense than any matter found on the Earth. As a white dwarf **cools** it **changes** into a **cold black dwarf** star.

The life of a star 2

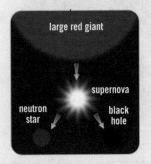

If a red giant star is massive enough it may have a slightly different future. It may, as it contracts, become unstable. An explosion then follows throwing dust and gas into space. An **exploding star** like this is called a **supernova**.

Any matter that is left behind after the explosion may form a **very dense neutron star or black hole**.

The gravitational field of a black hole is so strong that even light is unable to escape.

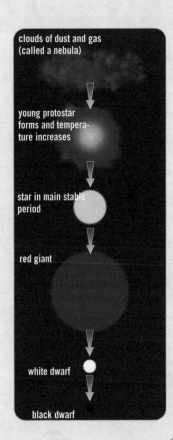

The origins of the universe

Our universe is **expanding**. We know this because when we look at the light spectra emitted by **distant galaxies** it shows **red shift**. Red shift occurs only if the **light source is moving away from us**. We also know from these spectra that the **further away a galaxy** is, the **greater the red shift**. This indicates that the **most distant** galaxies are **moving away from us at the greatest speeds**.

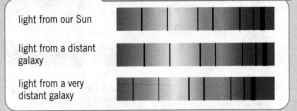

Spectra from galaxies showing red shift when compared with the spectrum from our Sun

light from our Sun

light from a distant galaxy

light from a very distant galaxy

All the above information leads scientists to believe that the **whole of the universe is expanding** and that in the beginning, **all the matter in the universe was in one place** which then **exploded**. This theory is called the **Big Bang Theory**.

Scientists have detected **background microwaves** in all parts of the Universe. They believe that this is the remains of the energy released during the Big Bang.

Scientists are now asking the question, 'will this expansion continue indefinitely or will gravity gradually slow it down and then, perhaps, reverse the process pulling all matter back to its place (**The Big Crunch**)?' Perhaps then there may be another explosion and the whole process begins again (**The Oscillating Model of the Universe**).

> *In most of the questions about the planets, stars and the universe, examiners are keen to see if students understand the importance of gravity. Make sure you understand the various stages in the birth and life of a star and how gravity is one of the main forces bringing about these changes.*

QUICK TEST

1. What is the name of our nearest star?

2. What is the name of the galaxy in which we live?

3. What forces bring together the particles of dust and gas to form a star?

4. What kinds of reaction cause the temperature of a forming star to increase?

5. What is the final stage in the life of a) a small star and b) a very large star?

6. When does a star or galaxy produce light with a red shift?

7. How was matter in the universe distributed in the beginning according to the big-bang theory?

8. Describe two possible futures for our Universe.

Exploring space

Apart from the Earth and the Moon, humans have not visited any of the other bodies in the universe. Nevertheless, we have lots of information about them. Much of this has come from observations made by *telescope* and *data collected by probes*.

Telescopes

Before the invention of telescopes, all human observations were done with the **unaided eye**. Our view of the universe was very limited. **Optical telescopes** greatly increased our abilities to see new astronomical bodies in our solar system, e.g. the moons of Jupiter and the outermost planets.

Keck Observatory on top of mountains in Hawaii

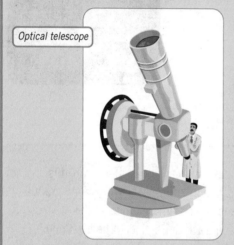

Optical telescope

Large optical telescopes, similar to the one shown, are often built on mountain tops. Here the images we see suffer less **distortions** from the **Earth's atmosphere** than those at sea level.

Another way to avoid these distortions is to mount **telescopes on satellites** which orbit the Earth high above its atmosphere. A good example of this is the **Hubble telescope** that was launched in 1990. It has seen **further into space** than any previous telescope.

This telescope is using radio waves to observe the night sky

Some modern telescopes use **other parts of the electromagnetic spectrum** to gather data. These include **radio waves, infrared and ultraviolet radiation**.

Probes

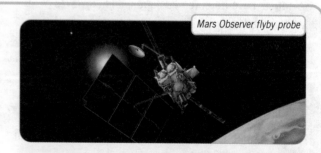

Mars Observer flyby probe

Flybys are unmanned probes that fly **close to or are put in orbit** around a planet or a moon in order **to gather information** which is then sent back to Earth.

Landers are unmanned probes which **land on the surface of a moon or planet**. They often carry out simple experiments, e.g. **testing soil samples, analysing the planet's or moon's atmosphere, gravitational or magnetic field**. They can provide more detailed information than the flyby probes but in general they are **far more expensive**.

The surface of Mars taken by Viking Lander

Manned missions

We could gather far more detailed information about our neighbouring astronomical bodies by sending manned probes but the **extra cost is enormous**. Most of this increase is due to the extra consideration which has to be given to **providing astronauts with an environment** that will keep them safe for the duration of the trip. It needs to cater for the following circumstances.

■ There is no **air/oxygen in space** so this must be taken with them. There is the possibility in the future that for longer journeys, plants could be grown on board a spacecraft to provide some of the oxygen necessary.

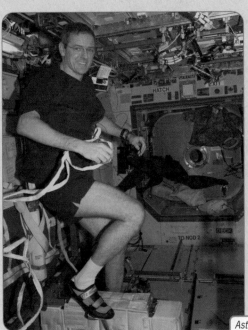

Astronaut in a space station exercising

■ Sufficient **water and food** must also be taken along. There is the hope that in the future perhaps some of this water may be found elsewhere in space, e.g. from comets.

■ There must be sufficient **fuel on board for the outward and the return journey**. There is no need for the return journey with an unmanned probe.

■ The Earth's atmosphere protects us from cosmic radiation, micrometeorites and much of the Sun's ultraviolet radiation. In space this will not be the case, so **radiation shields** will need to be included in the spacecraft's design.

■ Gravity during a journey in space will be much less than that on Earth. In fact, for most of the time astronauts are likely to experience **weightlessness**. This can have serious long-term effects on their health. Because astronauts have to do far less work against gravity, this is likely to lead to a) **calcium depletion** which may cause bones to become brittle and b) **muscle wastage**. The effects of both of these may be overcome by astronauts **exercising daily** during the journey or providing them with 'artificial gravity'.

Temperatures in space can vary enormously from −270°C to in excess of 200°C. A very narrow temperature range (approximately 10 to 30°C) needs to be maintained for manned flights. Maintaining this range will require energy, i.e. for cooling or heating.

The benefits of exploring space

Exploring space is very costly, but there have been many spin-offs or benefits. These include smoke detectors, weather and communication satellites, space blankets, flat panel TVs, high-power batteries for cordless tools, PTFE, mobile phones, ultrasound scanners, in car navigation systems and air traffic control collision avoidance systems.

QUICK TEST

1. Why are some telescopes built on top of mountains?

2. Explain the difference between a flyby probe and a lander. Give one example of each.

3. Give four reasons why manned flights are much more expensive than unmanned flights.

4. Give four spin-offs or benefits there have been from the exploration of space.

Practice questions

Use the questions to test your progress. Check your answers on page 126.

1. A crane uses 500 J of electrical energy to give a crate 300 J of gravitational potential energy. Calculate the efficiency of the crane. Suggest where the other 200 J of energy goes.

   ....

2. What is a thermogram? Give one use for a thermogram.

   ....

3. To which part of an electrical appliance should the Earth wire be connected?

   ....

4. What is a light-dependent resistor? Name one use for a light-dependent resistor.

   ....

5. State three ways in which the speed of rotation of a motor could be increased.

   ....

6. Calculate the electrical energy used in units when a 2 kW fire is turned on for three hours. Calculate the cost of this energy if the cost of one unit is 11p.

   ....

7. How much current flows through a 60 W bulb when it is connected to a 240 V supply?

   ....

8. Calculate the power of a hairdryer which when connected to a 240V supply has a current of 5 A flowing through it.

   ....

9. Calculate the current that will flow through a 12 Ω resistor if a p.d. of 6V is applied across its ends.

   ....

10. Calculate the p.d. across the ends of a 20 Ω resistor when a current of 0.5 A is flowing through it.

    ....

11. Calculate the resistance of a piece of wire when a p.d. of 6 V is applied across its ends allowing a current of 0.25 A to flow through it.

    ....

12. When a 3 kW fire is connected to an a.c. supply a current of 12.5 A flows. Calculate the voltage of the a.c. supply.

    ....

13. Calculate the correct fuse that should be included in a three-pin plug for a 1000 W 240 V hairdryer.

    ....

14. The diagram below shows the electromagnetic spectrum.

A	Microwaves	Infrared	Visible light	Ultraviolet	X-rays	B

a) Name the groups of waves A and B. ....

b) Name three properties which are common to all members of the electromagnetic spectrum.
....

c) Name two differences between the groups A and B. ....

d) Name two groups that could be used for cooking. ....

e) Name three groups that could be used for communicating. ....

f) Name two groups that could cause cancer. ....

g) Name one group used for seeing bones inside the body. ....

15. Calculate the speed of sound through a solid if a sound wave has a wavelength of 4 m and a frequency of 750 Hz.
....

16. Which of the three different types of radioactivity:

a) is not affected by a magnetic field? ....

b) carries a negative charge? ....

c) creates lots of ions as it travels through matter? ....

d) travels at the speed of light in a vacuum? ....

17. What is a satellite? Give one example of a) a natural satellite and b) an artificial satellite.
....

18. What is a supernova?
....

19. Who is likely to wear a radiation badge or dosimeter and what does it do?
....

20. What forces cause a star to become smaller? What creates the forces which cause a star to expand?
....

21. Name four ways in which we collect information about our universe.
....

22. Name three medical uses for radioisotopes.
....

23. Name two industrial uses for radioisotopes.
....

24. What piece of information suggests that all the stars and galaxies in the universe are moving away from each other at high speeds? Which theory of the beginning of the universe does this information support?
....

25. Why is a source of alpha radiation outside the body unlikely to cause damage to vital organs inside the body?
....

Answers

Biology
Quick test answers

Page 5 A balanced diet and nutrition
1. Energy
2. Starch and glucose
3. Store energy, make cell membranes and insulation
4. Repair and replace cells, and make new cells for growth
5. It helps food move through your system and prevents constipation
6. Saturated fats
7. Polyunsaturated fats
8. Fats

Page 7 The nervous system
1. Skin, tongue, eyes, ears, nose
2. Central nervous system
3. The brain, nerves, spinal cord
4. Sensory, relay and motor
5. A gap between neurones that transmits the nerve impulse
6. Sensory neurone
7. Motor neurone
8. Relay neurone
9. A change in the environment
10. They protect us from harm

Page 9 The eye
1. Iris
2. Pupil
3. Retina
4. It gets smaller
5. It gets larger
6. Ciliary muscles
7. Binocular vision is where the eyes are on the front of the head; in monocular, the eyes are on the side
8. Fat and round
9. Thin and flat
10. The cornea

Page 11 The brain
1. Cerebral cortex
2. Medulla
3. Epilepsy
4. When the blood supply to the brain is stopped
5. It affects the transmission of impulses across synapses by preventing the removal of serotonin

Page 13 Causes of disease
1. Virus, bacteria and fungi
2. Pathogens or germs
3. Destroy living tissue and produce toxins
4. They reproduce inside living cells and kill them
5. Athlete's foot and ringworm
6. By contact, air, and food and drink
7. An organism that transports a disease from person to person, e.g. mosquito
8. Via skin, digestive, reproductive and respiratory systems; and vectors (any three)

Page 15 Defence against disease
1. It is a barrier and produces an antiseptic oil
2. It traps dust and germs
3. Phagocytes and lymphocytes
4. Antitoxins and antibodies
5. Destroy toxins

6. Attach to antigens and clump germs together for the phagocytes to engulf
7. Dead or weak forms of a disease
8. Antibiotics are used to treat bacterial infections: continual use make bacteria resistant, so new forms of antibiotic are needed

Page 17 Drugs
1. Brain, liver and nervous system
2. Drugs that speed up the nervous system
3. Tar, nicotine and carbon monoxide
4. Emphysema, bronchitis, lung cancer and heart disease
5. Cirrhosis
6. Suppress pain sensors in the brain
7. Sedatives

Page 19 Hormones and diabetes
1. Adrenal glands
2. Pituitary gland
3. Maintaining the body at normal levels, making constant adjustments
4. Insulin and glucagon
5. Convert it to glycogen for storage
6. Glucagon
7. Insulin
8. Pancreas not producing enough insulin
9. Attention to diet and injections of insulin

Page 21 The menstrual cycle
1. Days 1–5
2. Lack of progesterone
3. Ovaries
4. Ovaries
5. Luteinising hormone/LH
6. Luteinising hormone/LH and follicle stimulating hormone/FSH
7. Development of an egg and release of oestrogen
8. Progesterone and oestrogen
9. Release of an egg
10. 28 days

Page 23 Genetics and variation
1. Homozygous
2. Genotype
3. Heterozygous
4. The weaker allele
5. The stronger allele
6. A fertilised egg
7. Sperms or eggs
8. The inheritance of one characteristic
9. All offspring/children will have blue eyes
10. BB or Bb

Page 25 Genetic engineering
1. A cow used to produce milk that contains antibodies and is low in cholesterol
2. DNA
3. Making human insulin or human growth hormone
4. The bacteria may mutate into harmful bacteria
5. Using genetic engineering to treat inherited diseases

Page 27 Inherited diseases
1. By a recessive allele passed on from two carrier parents
2. Thick, sticky mucus, difficulty breathing, frequent infections
3. By physiotherapy and strong antibiotics
4. One in four
5. Unspecialised cells
6. In bone marrow, human embryos and umbilical cords
7. To treat diseases and organ failure
8. Uncontrolled, jerky movements, depression
9. Caused by a dominant gene and sufferers have children before they realise they have it

Page 29 Selective breeding
1. Breeding animals or plants to produce the best offspring
2. In artificial selection, humans do the selecting, rather than nature
3. Genetically identical individuals
4. Embryo transfer and artificial insemination
5. Taking cuttings and tissue culture

Page 31 Pyramids
1. Energy is lost along the way
2. The numbers of organisms involved in a food chain
3. The mass of the organisms
4. Pyramids of biomass
5. The sun
6. 10%
7. They need to keep warm
8. Lost in respiration, urine and faeces
9. Respiration, heat, waste and parts of the body not eaten
10. Eat lower down in the food chain and intensively rear animals

Page 33 Evolution
1. Darwin and Lamarck
2. Darwin's
3. Environmental change, competition, disease and predators
4. The best adapted
5. Natural selection/survival of the fittest
6. The ground changed from marshy land to hard ground
7. The dark form: camouflaged against predators

Page 35 Adaptation and competition
1. Where an organism lives
2. The living things in a habitat
3. Animals or plants
4. Food, water and space
5. Light, space, water and nutrients
6. Also increase at first
7. Because of the predator–prey cycle
8. White (camouflage), thick (insulation) and greasy (does not hold water)
9. Enables it to lose heat to its surroundings
10. Only the best-adapted organisms will survive

Page 37 Environmental damage 1
1. Problems in food chains
2. Cutting down of trees and forests
3. Less carbon dioxide is being absorbed
4. Soil erosion, less rainfall and destruction of habitats
5. Manure

Page 39 Environmental damage 2
1. Burning fossil fuels
2. Sulphur dioxide and nitrogen oxides
3. Damage to buildings, plants, fish and birds
4. Increasing amounts of carbon dioxide and methane trapping too much heat
5. Use alternative energy sources and reduce the use of cars
6. CFCs
7. Lead

Page 41 Ecology and classification
1. Pooters and pitfall traps
2. Physical factors in a habitat such as temperature and soil pH
3. The habitat
4. Carl Linnaeus
5. Familiaris

Page 42 Answers to practice questions
1. An animal or plant that can indicate whether pollution is present in water or the air
2. Battery farming, fish farming, hydroponics (any one)
3. Autotroph
4. Dolly was the first mammal to be cloned
5. Mendel discovered the principles of genetics using pea plants
6. By breathing in the bacteria when the infected person coughs or sneezes
7. Contact lenses, glasses with concave lenses or cornea surgery
8. Active immunity is when the body fights off a disease with its own antibodies made by the white blood cells
9. A rise in blood cholesterol leading to increase risk of heart disease
10. Central Nervous System; it consists of brain, spinal cord and neurones
11. Relay, sensory and motor
12. Epilepsy
13. Insulin
14. a) Lower blood sugar levels to normal
    b) Raise blood sugar levels to normal
15. Banting and Best
16. An organism that transports a pathogen from one organism to another, e.g. a mosquito
17. Phagocytes and lymphocytes
18. Natural immunity is when the body can remember a disease and produce antibodies to fight it before any symptoms develop
19. The body maintaining a constant internal environment

20. Recessive – cystic fibrosis. Dominant – Huntington's chorea
21. Alleles
22. FSH, LH, oestrogen and progesterone
23. Bacteria
24. The numbers and mass of organisms involved in a food chain
25. Charles Darwin
26. Lamarck
27. Urine and faeces, respiration, movement, growth, decomposition
28. Quadrats, pooters and pitfall traps
29. Classification
30. A group of living things able to breed together to produce fertile offspring

Chemistry
Quick test answers
Page 45 Limestone
1. Calcium carbonate
2. Sedimentary
3. Igneous
4. Neutralises acidity in lakes and soils
5. zinc carbonate → zinc oxide + carbon dioxide
6. $ZnCO_3(s) \rightarrow ZnO(s) + CO_2(g)$
7. Roasting clay and limestone
8. Heating limestone, sand and soda
9. Sodium carbonate, carbon dioxide and water
10. $2NaHCO_3 \rightarrow Na_2CO_3 + CO_2 + H_2O$

Page 47 Fuels
1. Coal, oil and natural gas
2. Millions of years
3. Hydrogen and carbon
4. Runny, easy to ignite and have low boiling points
5. Short-chain ones
6. At the top
7. They are more useful
8. Hot aluminium oxide
9. Alkenes
10. A group of compounds with a similar number of carbon atoms

Page 49 Organic families
1. Four
2. 'Saturated' means no double bonds; 'hydrocarbons' contain hydrogen and carbon atoms only
3. Methane
4.
```
    H                H  H
    |                |  |
H - C - H      H -  C - C - H
    |                |  |
    H                H  H

  H  H  H          H  H  H  H
  |  |  |          |  |  |  |
H-C--C--C-H    H - C--C--C--C-H
  |  |  |          |  |  |  |
  H  H  H          H  H  H  H
```
5.
```
  H        H      H  H
   \      /       |  |
    C = C     H - C = C - C - H
   /      \              |
  H        H             H
```
6. Alkenes
7. Alkenes decolourise bromine water while alkanes do not react
8. C_nH_{2n+2}
9. Alcohols
10. C_2H_5OH

Page 51 Vegetable oils
1. Fruits, seeds and nuts
2. Seeds
3. Vitamins A and D
4. Fats can reach much higher temperatures than water
5. Fried
6. Saturated

7. Lots of C=C bonds
8. They can be spread and used to make products like cakes and pastries
9. Nickel
10. To reduce the amount of sugar needed

Page 53 Plastics
1.
$$n \quad \begin{array}{c} H \\ \\ C = C \\ \\ H \end{array} \begin{array}{c} H \\ \\ \\ \\ H \end{array} \rightarrow \left(\begin{array}{ccc} H & & H \\ | & & | \\ -C & - & C- \\ | & & | \\ H & & H \end{array} \right)_n$$
2.
$$n \quad \begin{array}{c} CH_3 \\ \\ C = C \\ \\ H \end{array} \begin{array}{c} H \\ \\ \\ \\ H \end{array} \rightarrow \left(\begin{array}{ccc} CH_3 & & H \\ | & & | \\ -C & - & C- \\ | & & | \\ H & & H \end{array} \right)_n$$
3. Addition polymerisation
4. Monomer
5. Thermosetting plastics
6. Thermosetting plastic
7. Polythene
8. Polypropene
9. Polypropene

Page 55 Ethanol
1. C_2H_5OH
2. Drinks, solvents and as a fuel
3. They could become blind or even die
4. A purple dye and an unpleasant taste
5. Bio-diesel
6. Yeast
7. $C_6H_{12}O_6$
8. It becomes denatured and stops working
9. Phosphoric acid
10. Ethene + steam → ethanol

Page 57 Evolution of the atmosphere
1. 20%
2. Nitrogen
3. Carbon dioxide, water vapour and noble gases
4. Carbon dioxide, steam, ammonia and methane
5. Carbon dioxide
6. Removed carbon dioxide and produced oxygen
7. Became locked up in sedimentary rocks and fossil fuels
8. Filters out harmful UV rays
9. New, more complex life forms could develop
10. Burning fossil fuels

Page 59 Pollution of the atmosphere
1. Sulphur dioxide
2. Coal
3. If less electricity is needed then fewer fossil fuels will be burnt
4. The flame will have a yellow colour
5. Carbon dioxide
6. Carbon monoxide
7. Smoke particles
8. A reduction in the amount of sunlight that reaches the Earth's surface which may even affect weather patterns
9. Carbon dioxide
10. Catalytic converter

Page 61 Pollution of the environment
1. Fertilisers
2. They are decomposed by bacteria, which use up the oxygen in the water
3. Stomach cancer and 'blue baby' disease
4. Bauxite
5. Rainforests
6. Recycle aluminium

7. The quarries can scar the landscape
8. It brings new jobs and money into the area
9. Non-biodegradable
10. Hydrogen chloride

Page 63 Evidence for plate tectonics
1. Crust
2. Solid
3. Silicon, oxygen and aluminium
4. Iron and nickel
5. A few centimetres per year
6. Crust and upper mantle
7. The Earth's surface shrank as it cooled
8. Natural radioactive decay
9. They fit together like pieces of a jigsaw
10. The remains of an unusual crocodile were found in rocks of a similar age on both sides of the Atlantic

Page 65 Consequences of plate tectonics
1. Past each other, towards each other or away from each other
2. When plates move past each other
3. There are too many factors involved
4. California, USA
5. The oceanic plate melts
6. Plates are moving past each other, lava can breakthrough the crust to form volcanoes
7. Iron
8. The Earth's magnetic field

Page 67 Extraction of iron
1. Gold
2. Heat with carbon
3. Electrolysis
4. Haematite
5. Iron ore, coke and limestone
6. Oxygen from hot air
7. Carbon monoxide
8. More dense
9. Slag
10. Road building and in fertilisers

Page 69 Iron and steel
1. Making steel
2. Water and oxygen
3. It stops water and oxygen reaching the iron
4. Magnesium or zinc (either one)
5. Carbon
6. Hard, strong, does not rust but is brittle
7. Wrought iron
8. The atoms have a very regular structure and so the layers can pass easily over each other
9. Carbon
10. Iron, chromium and nickel

Page 71 Aluminium
1. Bauxite
2. It is soft and has a low density
3. An alloy
4. It is protected by a layer of aluminium oxide
5. Al_2O_3
6. Electrolysis
7. Oxide ions
8. Aluminium ions
9. Carbon, graphite
10. They react with oxygen to form carbon dioxide

Page 73 Titanium
1. By alloying it with other metals
2. Titanium quickly reacts with oxygen to form a layer of titanium dioxide that stops any further reactions

3. To make replacement joints
4. Rutile
5. Titanium dioxide
6. Beaches
7. Because titanium is more reactive than carbon
8. Magnesium
9. Titanium chloride + magnesium → titanium + magnesium chloride
10. Nickel and titanium

Page 75 Copper
1. Chalcopyrite and chalcosine
2. Sulphur dioxide
3. By leaching it from low grade ores
4. Electrolysis
5. $Cu - 2e^- \rightarrow Cu^{2+}$
6. $Cu^{2+} + 2e^- \rightarrow Cu$
7. The negative electrode
8. Alloys
9. Copper and tin
10. Copper and zinc

Page 77 Transition metals
1. Free electrons
2. Middle section
3. High melting point, high density, shiny, tough, hard wearing, form coloured compounds and are good catalysts
4. Good electrical conductor which can be bent
5. Does not corrode or fracture
6. Iron is brittle
7. Bridges, buildings, ships, cars and trains
8. Haber process
9. Coins
10. Margarine

Page 79 The noble gases
1. They have a full outer shell of electrons
2. Increases
3.

4.

5. Individual atoms
6. Balloons and airships
7. It is less dense than air and it is not flammable
8. Electrical discharge tubes
9. Filament light bulbs
10. Lasers

Page 81 Chemical tests
1. When this gas is bubbled through limewater, it turns the limewater cloudy
2. The gas bleaches damp litmus paper
3. The gas turns damp blue litmus paper red
4. Bromine water turns from brown to colourless
5. Carbon dioxide
6. Green
7. Lilac
8. Apple green
9. White
10. Pale blue

Page 82 Answers to practice questions
1. a) Limestone/marble/chalk
   b) Calcium oxide/carbon dioxide
   c) $Ca(OH)_2$
   d) Glass

2. a) CH_4
   b) Ethane
   c) Alkanes
   d) C_2H_4
   e) Propene
   f) Alkenes
3. a) Fractional distillation
   b) More flammable
   c) Cracking
4.
```
    H  H  H  H
    |  |  |  |
 H--C--C--C--C--H
    |  |  |  |
    H  H  H  H
```
5. a) Alloy
   b) Iron, chromium and nickel
   c) Carbon
6. a) A sketch showing atoms of the same size in a regular arrangement.
   b) A sketch showing atoms of two or more different sizes not in a regular arrangement.
   c) In the titanium alloy the layers of atoms cannot pass easily over each other.
7. c, a, d, b
8. a) Lithium chloride
   b) Copper carbonate
   c) Zinc carbonate
   d) Potassium chloride
9. a) oxygen
   b) chlorine
   c) hydrogen
   d) ammonia

Physics
Quick test answers
Page 85 Energy
1. Heat (or thermal), light, sound, electrical, chemical, kinetic, elastic or strain potential, gravitational potential, nuclear (any five)
2. Electric fire, electric bell, loudspeaker, electric motor (any three of these or similar)
3. Gravitational potential energy
4. Electrical to heat, kinetic and sound
5. None

Page 87 Generating electricity
1. Coal, oil and gas
2. Carbon dioxide
3. Coal and oil
4. Oil spillage
5. They cannot be replaced
6. More efficient insulation and engines; use more renewable sources of energy (any two of these)

Page 89 Renewable sources of energy
1. Hydroelectricity, tidal, wave
2. Wind and waves
3. Wind and biomass
4. Geothermal and tidal
5. Wind

Page 91 Heat transfer–conduction
1. Allows heat to flow through it
2. Metal; saucepan (or other suitable example and use)
3. Does not allow heat through it
4. Plastic; tablemat (or other suitable example and use)
5. Two panes of glass with air in-between
6. Insulation in loft, double glazing, draft excluders carpets and underlay, cavity wall insulation

Page 93 Heat transfer–convection
1. It becomes less dense
2. It becomes more dense and falls

3. Too much energy is lost up the chimney
4. To prevent heat loss by convection
5. It should be at the top of the compartment
6. Hot air will rise from the beach, so an onshore breeze will blow

Page 95 Heat transfer–radiation
1. Electromagnetic radiation or infrared waves
2. Because conduction and convection require particles - only radiation can travel through a vacuum
3. Absorbed or reflected
4. Dark and rough
5. Light-coloured and smooth
6. A photograph taken using the radiation emitted by an object
7. Dark and rough
8. Light-coloured and smooth
9. Black

Page 97 Effects of heat transfer
1. 4.2 kJ of energy is needed to increase the temperature of 1 kg of water by 1°C
2. 42 kJ
3. 23 kJ
4. 2.4 MJ of energy is needed to change 1 kg of water at 100°C to steam at 100°C
5. 24 MJ
6. 340 kJ of energy is needed to change 1 kg of ice at 0°C into water at the same temperature
7. 1.02 MJ

Page 99 Current, charge and resistance
1. Flow of charge
2. a) ammeter
   b) voltmeter
3. 4.5 Ω
4. Thermistor. Fire alarm.

Page 101 Electrical power
1. a) 6000 J,
   b) 150 kJ,
   c) 72 kJ,
   d) 240 kJ,
   e) 600 kJ
2. a) 9 units,
   b) 1 unit,
   c) 3 units,
   d) 2 units,
   e) 1 unit
3. 3 kW

Page 103 Motors and generators
1. Split ring/commutator
2. Increase the current in the coil, increase the number of turns on the coil and increase the strength of the magnets
3. Smoother turning and more powerful
4. Alternating current
5. Increase the speed of rotation, increase the strength of the magnetic field, increase the number of turns on the alternator's coil (any two)

Page 105 Domestic electricity
1. a.c.
2. a) brown,
   b) green and yellow and
   c) blue
3. Very good conductors
4. Can be reset
5. When using an electric lawn mower or hedge trimmers

Page 107 Waves
1. Energy

2. 25 waves produced by source each second
3. a) Light waves
   b) Sound waves
4. 15 m/s
5. P-waves and S-waves
6. P-waves: transverse, faster, can travel through liquids. S-waves: longitudinal, slower, cannot travel through liquids
7. S-waves cannot travel through it

Page 109 The electromagnetic spectrum
1. Travel through vacuum at the speed of light transverse
2. Radio, microwave, visible
3. Ultraviolet, X-ray and gamma
4. Visible light and infrared

Page 111 Analogue and digital signals
1. It strikes the sides at angles greater than the critical angle and so is totally internally reflected
2. Cheaper, lighter, carry more signals, more secure (any three)
3. As they travel they get weaker and so must be amplified
4. Unwanted distortions that are 'picked up' by a signal as it travels
5. Noise alters the shape of an analogue signal
6. The distortions of the signal caused by the noise are amplified
7. The received signal may be very different from the original
8. The final signal received is a perfect copy of the original

Page 113 Nuclear radiations
1. a) gamma,
   b) alpha,
   c) beta,
   d) beta,
   e) gamma

Page 115 Uses of radioactivity
1. a) beta and
   b) gamma
2. Tracer
3. Cell damage due to alpha radiation
4. Radiotherapy
5. Gamma
6. The creation of ions by the alpha emitter

Page 117 The Earth in space
1. a) The Sun,
   b) The moon and the planets (either)
2. Gravitational forces
3. When they are closest to the Sun
4. A near Earth object. A large NEO, such as an asteroid, could destroy the life on Earth
5. A moon
6. Looking into space, weather and communications

Page 119 Stars and the universe
1. The Sun
2. The Milky Way
3. Gravitational forces
4. Nuclear fusion reactions
5. a) Black dwarf and
   b) supernova and black hole/neutron star
6. When it is moving away from us
7. All in one place
8. It continues to expand. It stops expanding and contracts (Big

Crunch). It may then explode and start to expand again (The Oscillating Universe).

Page 121 Exploring space
1. To avoid distortions caused by the Earth's atmosphere
2. Flyby probes do not land. Deep Space 1 is a flyby probe. The Viking2 Lander landed on Mars.
3. Need to take food, water and oxygen; need a constant temperature; protection from radiation; and enough fuel for return
4. Smoke detectors, weather and communication satellites, space blankets, flat panel TVs, high-power batteries for cordless tools, PTFE, mobile phones (any four, or similar)

Page 122 Answers to practice questions
1. 60%. Lost as heat to the surroundings
2. A picture which shows different temperatures as different colours. Used to find places where heat is escaping from a building
3. The outer casing
4. A resistor whose resistance decreases in bright light. Controlling street lights
5. Larger current, more turns on coil, stronger magnetic field
6. 6 units, 66p
7. 0.25 A
8. 1200 W
9. 0.5 A
10. 40 V
11. 24 Ω
12. 240 V
13. 5 A
14. a) A is radio waves and B is gamma waves
    b) They can all be reflected, refracted and undergo diffraction. They all travel at the same speed in a vacuum
    c) Gamma waves have shorter wavelengths and larger frequencies,
    d) Microwaves and infrared waves,
    e) Microwaves, radio waves, and visible light,
    f) ultraviolet waves, gamma waves and X-rays (any two),
    g) X-rays
15. 3000 m/s
16. a) Gamma,
    b) Beta,
    c) Alpha,
    d) Gamma
17. An object that orbits a planet, a) the Moon, b) a weather satellite
18. An exploding star
19. Someone who works with radioactive materials. A dosimeter measure the amount of radiation he or she has been exposed to
20. Gravitational forces. Expansive forces are caused by heating
21. The naked eye, telescopes, flyby probes and landers
22. Radiotherapy, sterilisation and radioactive tracers (bloodstream)
23. Quality control, food preservation, radioactive tracers (pipes) (any two)
24. Red shift, big-bang theory
25. Alpha radiation cannot penetrate skin

Index